In *CONSULTAT...*
YOUR PSYCHO...
You'll Find Ans...
to Questions Li...

How does psychotherapy work to help me?
How do I know if I need psychotherapy?
What can I do about my problems if I don't want to go for therapy?
How do I know if a therapist is right for me?
How can I get someone I care about to go for therapy?

And How to Deal With:

• Relationships: work, friends, lovers • Family and job problems • Moods, fears, anxieties • Addictions • Sexual difficulties • Compulsions and obsessions • Psychosomatic disorders • Life crises

———————

DR. ELLIOTT SELIGMAN is a New York State licensed clinical psychologist. He is on the faculty of the National Institute for Psychotherapies, and coordinates the Institute's Behavioral Psychotherapy and Sex Therapy Program.

NANCY BRUNING is a writer who specializes in consumer-oriented health topics. She has written several books, including *COPING WITH CHEMOTHERAPY*.

CONSULTATION WITH YOUR PSYCHOTHERAPIST

ELLIOTT SELIGMAN, Ph.D.,
with NANCY BRUNING

PUBLISHED BY POCKET BOOKS NEW YORK

Another *Original* publication of POCKET BOOKS

POCKET BOOKS, a division of Simon & Schuster, Inc.,
1230 Avenue of the Americas, New York, N.Y. 10020

ISBN: 0-671-54335-0

First Pocket Books Printing June, 1986

10 9 8 7 6 5 4 3 2 1

POCKET and colophon are registered trademarks
of Simon & Schuster, Inc.

Printed in the U.S.A.

Contents

PART ONE

The Basics of Psychotherapy

CHAPTER ONE

Understanding Psychotherapy

I've heard so many different things about psychotherapy. I'm very confused. What is psychotherapy?

Psychotherapy is a general term used to describe a wide range of methods used to treat emotional problems. At times it may seem as if there are almost as many definitions of psychotherapy as there are psychotherapists. All these definitions, however, have one idea in common: psychotherapy involves change. When you enter psychotherapy, you begin a relationship with another person (the therapist) who has the expertise to help you go through the process of change in which you'll explore, improve, and better understand yourself—your thoughts, feelings, and behavior.

A friend of mine went for counseling at her company because she was having trouble getting along with her boss. Is psychotherapy the same as counseling?

No—although there may be some overlap. Counseling involves a counselor giving specific advice to help a person with an individual situation (such as an interpersonal conflict at work). The idea behind therapy, on the other hand, is to teach people how to cope with and resolve life's problems on their own, rather than to depend on someone's advice for every new problem that crops up.

Counseling may appear at first to be more attractive than psychotherapy, and may prove helpful to some in the short run. In general, however, counseling provides only temporary solutions, whereas psychotherapy seeks to provide individuals with more long-lasting relief from their problems. Therapists believe that people fall into and repeat basic patterns; we keep thinking, feeling, and doing the same types of things over and over again. A therapist tries to understand these overall patterns. Then, through various means that are explained in the next chapter, the therapist tries to help the patient change those patterns by helping that individual to understand the inner self. As a result of the relearning that comes about through therapy, a person is better equipped to deal with present—and future—problems instead of being overwhelmed by them.

I've always discussed my problems with my close pals at work. How is psychotherapy different from talking to friends and relatives?

This is a very common question asked of therapists, and it's true that we're all influenced to some extent by our relationships with others. But their effect upon us is always changing, it may not be positive, and it tends to be superficial. No matter how intelligent your friends and relatives are, or how much they want to help you, they are neither specially trained nor objective enough to be truly effective in getting you to make positive changes in your life. They tend to see things from their own personal points of view. They also have a stake in maintaining their roles in your life, and sometimes will not want to jeopardize those roles or relationships.

Unlike your friends and relatives, the psychotherapist has the expertise to influence and affect you in an intense, basic, directed, positive, relatively fast, and permanent way. And while the therapist is interested in your welfare, he or she is not personally involved with you. The therapist has a much clearer view and a less personal stake in what to say to you or how to say it than a friend or relative might. Furthermore, you will more likely feel free about candidly discussing any and all issues in therapy—such openness would be unlikely with friends or relatives.

My daughter in college has been telling me that I should go for psychotherapy for my problems. I think she's the crazy one. Isn't psychotherapy just for people who are having a nervous breakdown?

Let's begin by talking about what you mean by "nervous breakdown." This is a commonly used term that covers a variety of psychiatric situations—including severe anxiety attacks, severe depression, suicide attempts, and psychosis—where the person loses touch with reality and suffers dramatic personality changes. It is usually used to describe a person who temporarily stops functioning in some significant way. The person may be a threat to himself or to others, and is frequently hospitalized in a psychiatric ward for at least a short period of time.

Although psychotherapy is helpful to people who have these extreme difficulties, the vast majority of people receiving psychotherapy do so on an outpatient basis, have never been hospitalized, and are not experiencing the severe psychiatric symptoms mentioned above. They just have problems and want someone to help them because they don't seem to be able to solve these problems on their own.

I've spent hours thinking about it and talking about it with my wife, but I'm still not sure what to do. I know I have emotional problems, but how do I know if I should start psychotherapy?

This is a difficult question to answer because problems often have more than one explanation. If you had a broken leg, for example, it would be obvious that you needed medical treatment. But psychotherapy is often not "needed" in the same way that medical treatment is needed. Therapy is a voluntary move you make to improve your life and to make you feel better. People usually enter therapy because they are somehow dissatisfied with the way things are. They are suffering some kind of discomfort—not physical discomfort necessarily, more likely mental or psychological discomfort. They may be experiencing difficulty in the way they relate to other people; they may just not be getting done the things they want to get done. Some people simply want to grow as persons—they feel "empty" or "flat"; they may lack purpose and direction, or sense that something is missing from their lives. If you are experiencing problems, you may want to consider entering therapy. You should remember, however, that *you* are really the only one who can make this decision.

Should I listen to others when they tell me I should or shouldn't have therapy?

Deciding to see a therapist is a very personal choice. Although you may want to listen to other people, and may begin therapy because someone suggests it, therapy works best if you believe it is right for you. You are the one who has to go through the actual process. Furthermore, you are the world's expert on yourself; no one knows how you feel as well as you do.

If you are considering therapy because someone has recommended it to you, remember to look at the motivation of that person. Does he or she really have *your* interests at heart? Is someone suggesting therapy for you because he wants you to change for him? Or are you hesitant about entering therapy because a friend finds it threatening for you? He or she may be afraid that the changes that will occur in your life as a result of therapy will hurt or destroy your friendship.

This is not to say that you should completely ignore other people's thoughts on this matter. Friends and relatives may have valuable insights and listening to their suggestions may give you a clue that it's time to examine your own needs, abilities, and desires, and perhaps to consider the question of entering therapy.

I've been through therapy and it helped me tremendously. I think my cousin should go into therapy too. How can I convince her that she needs—and can get—help?

The first step for anyone in this position to take is to examine the reasons why he or she wants another person to start therapy. If you only want your cousin to change so you can get along with her better, or like her more, make that clear. If you truly care about her happiness, you should express that in an honest way; if seeing her sad really makes you sad, let her know it, and that you think therapy might help. If she is considering therapy but is procrastinating, you can stress the fact that therapy is something she can just try—if it doesn't work out, she can always quit. But remember that ultimately, of course, the choice lies in her hands and you should respect her decision.

Why do people have so many problems today? My parents and grandparents seemed to get along fine without any professional help.

This is a commonly asked question with a number of possible answers.

• *More Possibilities* Today there are many possibilities open to us in the areas of career, lifestyle, choice of mate, financial success, and personal beliefs. As a result, there is more confusion, disappointment, and dissatisfaction. Divorce has become socially acceptable to the point where even the president of the country can be divorced. As the divorce rate skyrockets, the number of people that experience psychological and emotional problems as a result of divorce has increased greatly. In addition, we now recognize certain women as being non-assertive. Before the advent of women's rights, this problem was frequently overlooked as women were encouraged to be non-assertive.

• *Fewer Informal Counselors* Society was structured quite differently in the old days. When people had problems, they turned to religious leaders or elder members of the family for counseling and advice. As close relationships with clergymen are no longer common and close-knit families have become a thing of the past, a need for professional counseling has been created.

• *People Did Suffer* A third explanation is that people may have suffered just as much in the past—but in silence. For instance, during my years in graduate school I was involved in setting up a mental health center in an extremely rural area of Appalachia in Kentucky. Although there were several physicians nearby, mental health services were unknown and unavailable. To these people, anyone with noticeable psychological difficulties was considered "funny" or "touched," and might be made fun of or ignored. Others, with less obvious problems, suffered privately. Officially, no one was being treated for a mental health problem until we got there—but that didn't mean there were no problems. Upon opening and advertising the center, people quickly applied for treatment.

There always seems to be the implication in this question that therapy creates problems where there are none. While this *may* occasionally occur in psychotherapy, I don't think it is true overall. Therapy gives many troubled people an alternative to suffering.

Before I invest my time and money I'd like a realistic picture of what psychotherapy can do for me. What can I expect?

People often hope that they will be able to have a few sessions of therapy, get some good advice, and walk away with their problems solved. Sometimes they get their wish by undergoing short-term therapy during times of crisis. Such therapy is quite beneficial to people who are experiencing a traumatic event, such as divorce, the death of a loved one, or a life-threatening illness. In these cases, therapy supports and guides a person through a particularly stressful period that would be very difficult to get through alone.

In most situations, however, it is more accurate and helpful to think of therapy as a long-term growth experience that allows you to be a fuller, more emotive, more capable person. The quality of your life can improve with therapy; you may find you are able to enjoy life more. By giving you the opportunity to understand yourself, to learn new ways of coping with your problems, and to express your feelings and needs with an expert who will not judge you, you can achieve a basic change in the way you think, feel, and act. This change may be very noticeable to others, or more subtle, but it will be highly noticeable to you. Except for the special short-term situations described above, it is almost always a gradual change.

What kinds of problems are helped by psychotherapy? Will it help me get rid of my depression and get along better with other people?

The list of problems that can be helped by psychotherapy is a long one. As a result of therapy, you may be able to cope better with problems such as depression, anxiety, personal and love relationships, destructive habits, phobias, nonasser- tiveness, procrastination, sexual problems, lack of self-es- teem, psychosomatic illness, and crises. These problems may be largely eradicated or reduced, depending on their severity. You must realize, however, that in all therapy a large share of the responsibility for change depends on the effort that *you* put into it.

I've heard about psychotherapy on TV and the radio for years. Sometimes I'm tempted to go, but I'm afraid of what other people will think of me. Does seeing a therapist mean that I'm weak or "crazy"?

Absolutely not. It may make you feel better to know that many "normal" people are secretly afraid of being crazy but do not admit it. In fact, psychotherapy is not limited to those with severe problems; most people in therapy are functioning reasonably well.

Unfortunately, a large number of people still attach a stigma to psychotherapy, under the misconception that peo- ple in therapy are sick, crazy, or weak—and if they weren't, they would be able to change on their own, or put up with their discomfort. Men, in particular, have more trouble making the decision to undergo therapy. They are trained to not allow themselves to ask for help or to express emotions to other people; they may see going for therapy as a sign of weakness. The same people who wouldn't hesitate to call upon the services of a lawyer, car mechanic, investment broker, heart surgeon, or other expert feel there is something wrong with consulting a psychotherapist. If people tease you about going into therapy, that is exactly what you should point out to them.

I know so many people who could benefit by therapy, but they never go. What are some of the reasons that people are so reluctant to enter psychotherapy?

Often, their reasons result from a lack of knowledge or are related to problems that, ironically, could be treated successfully in therapy. People are afraid that therapy will be painful or unpleasant—that they will find out things about themselves that they don't want to. Therapy may indeed be painful at times, but so is removing a splinter from your foot. You could probably leave it there and continue to limp along with the dull pain. Pulling it out may hurt more at the time, but afterward the cause of the pain is gone and you can begin the healing process.

In addition, the people you've talked to may doubt that psychotherapy works. They may be scared by the possibility that if it doesn't work for them, they could be left without a shred of hope. They may think: If therapy fails, what's left? So they deny their problems, or they think about going, but never get around to it. Others are just hesitant to try something they know little about. Still others have the misconception that they will become overly dependent on a therapist and never leave therapy; when therapy is working well, this is not the case.

There are many things I don't like about myself and want to change. But I'm afraid therapy will change me into someone I like even less. Will therapy change me into someone else?

The answer here is a definitive "no." People fear that if they admit that they wish to change, and then allow themselves to be open to such changes, they'll somehow be swept away. In my experience, not only does this not happen, but the problem in therapy is quite the reverse. You are rarely in danger of being dramatically transformed in an unacceptable way. It's true that on occasion, after a particular therapy session, you may feel very different. But what usually happens is that over a brief period of time, that "different" feeling drifts away, and you come close to re-establishing your usual sense of self. The greatest problem in therapy, then, is that there is so much resistance to change that you will not change *enough*.

I don't think I'm ready for psychotherapy; besides, it would be a real financial burden to me right now. What can I do on my own before I try therapy?

Although self-help is sometimes limited in its effectiveness, there are several measures you might want to try before entering therapy.

1. First, you can try to become aware of some of the underlying causes of the thoughts, feelings, and behavior you wish to change. You may then be able to gradually reduce such undesirable behavior or thought patterns. In Part Two of this book, we'll be pointing out some of the major underlying causes of common emotional problems.

2. There are many self-help books that suggest programs you can try to apply to yourself. However, reading these books may not be enough. Even though self-help books may cover the important points, you may need someone to interact with. Overcoming your problems almost always involves changing your own belief or attitude about yourself or others.

In order for such changes to become stable forces in our lives, we usually need someone to challenge our way of thinking. A therapist can act as this "someone." Too often, we can distort what has been happening in our lives in order to come up with a particular, desired explanation for our problems. And we may not even realize it till someone else questions our way of thinking or "story" at the right time and in the right way. In addition, self-help books cannot address the particularities of our problems the way another individual can.

3. You might want to try self-help groups, which are less formal and more directed than individual therapy. For example, there are groups for weight loss, alcoholism, and compulsive gambling. These usually contain elements of psychotherapy, but can give you even more of a sense of support and camaraderie, since everyone is in the same boat. However, there is usually a lack of individualized treatment. In addition, you will be more likely to encounter group disapproval and pressure if you "slip" in a self-help group than in individual therapy.

4. Many people attempt to relax or to escape their problems by not dealing with them directly, or by preoccupying themselves with diversions. If you do this, you may find temporary relief, but be aware that these means of relief may in themselves become problems, especially when the escape is in the form of drugs or alcohol.

If you try self-help first, remember: *you can't start too small* when you're trying to overcome a particular problem. Progress is made in inches. Also, don't fall into the trap of evaluating yourself by comparing yourself with other people. You are where you are—it's true that other people may not have your problems, but the chances are they have some other problems that may be as troubling as yours. However, even if this is not so, it doesn't mean you can't or shouldn't make the effort to change your life. Reward yourself when you see some improvement, no matter how small. The reward may be treating yourself to something tangible—a movie, a massage, a book, or just mentally patting yourself on the back. And above all, don't put yourself down because of your problems, or because you don't see any progress. You are experiencing enough difficulty without adding guilt and self-hatred to your problems.

I've only just realized how deeply my psychological problems are affecting my entire life. Is it possible for my problems to go away by themselves eventually? Or might they get worse if I don't get help?

Yes, to your first question. Time may be another alternative to therapy—sometimes it's true that "time heals all wounds." So you may choose to wait things out a bit to see what happens. But be careful not to fool yourself. As months and years go by, you may still be telling yourself that all you need is a little more time.

As to your second question, if time *doesn't* solve your problems, it doesn't necessarily mean they'll get worse. They *may* get worse, but they may stay the same or even improve a little. No matter what happens, however, there is also the choice not to go into therapy. You may decide that you are just going to live in your present state. This choice has to be respected if it is an informed decision.

While I don't think anyone should go into therapy without expecting to put some effort into getting through the rough times that lie ahead, therapy is not necessarily a lifetime or even a years-long commitment. I tell my patients to look at therapy not as stepping off a cliff, but as taking the first step down a road. Once you've decided to try therapy, you can always decide to stop.

CHAPTER TWO

Schools of Psychotherapy and How They Work

The Major Schools

Every time I turn around, they're talking about a new type of psychotherapy. What are the various forms or schools of psychotherapy?

There are literally hundreds of different schools of psychotherapy. Each school, or approach, is based on some overall view of human nature—each has its own theory on how the human mind works, how we develop problems, and how to treat those problems. However, most therapists practice one form of these three general approaches: psychoanalytic, cognitive-behavioral, or Gestalt therapy.

What is the psychoanalytic approach? I keep hearing about psychoanalysis.

Sigmund Freud, the founder of psychoanalytic treatment, believed that adults and children are motivated by instinct—our needs and desires—especially the sexual instinct. What we want and what society deems acceptable, however, are often two different things. So conflicts arise inside us between our desire to satisfy those drives and our desire to live comfortably in our society.

If, as we mature, we are not able to resolve those conflicts—either by curbing our drives or by expressing them in some indirect, acceptable way—emotional problems develop. The problems continue to plague us in one form or another until the conflict is resolved. A classic Freudian example of this is the Oedipus Complex, in which it is believed that the maturing male child experiences a sexual attraction for his mother and suffers the consequent anger and fear of his father. In our society, of course, this is not acceptable in thought or deed; this powerful conflict must somehow be resolved in the child's mind.

I've read that psychoanalysis has changed over the years. Is this true?

Though there have been many modifications in Freud's original theory, most modern practitioners of psychoanalysis still believe that early childhood experiences give rise to the unconscious conflicts that are at the root of emotional problems. Psychoanalysis therefore involves encouraging you to explore underlying conflicts, giving you insight into how your present behavior reflects these conflicts and helping you to resolve them. Analysts believe that once your inner conflicts are in the open the symptoms that brought you into therapy will disappear naturally.

What are the behavioral and cognitive-behavioral approaches? I've heard so little about them.

The behavioral approach was originally based on the "learning theory," which developed from the results of experiments with animals. Researchers demonstrated that since behavior was learned, undesirable problem behavior could be unlearned and replaced by new, desirable behavior patterns. Early practitioners dealt mostly with observable problems such as phobias, muscle tics, and outbursts of anger.

As with the psychoanalytic approach, there have been many changes in the behavioral therapy, though a few strict behaviorists still practice. Most now belong to the cognitive-behavioral school of thought. This acknowledges "cognition"—the way we perceive and understand something—as a primary influence in behavior. These cognitions are some-

21

times subconscious—thoughts we may not be aware of. The way an event is perceived may vary greatly from person to person, and many people have been brought up to believe what cognitive-behaviorists consider irrational, self-defeating, or irrelevant thought patterns.

Cognitive-behavior modification (CBM) is an approach to psychotherapy that focuses not only on the outside, observable behavior, but on catching the conscious or unconscious thought that leads to that behavior. If we change the way a person perceives something, we'll change his feelings and subsequent behavior. Many of the self-help suggestions that you'll find in this book and in others are CBM-oriented.

My friend is undergoing Gestalt therapy and is always asking me about my feelings. What is Gestalt therapy?

The notion here is that people are born wonderful, happy creatures and would remain that way if allowed to grow up naturally. It is society, which begins to influence us as children, that sometimes pushes us onto the wrong track. According to Gestalt theory, our problems occur when we absorb other people's value-judgments. When these value-judgments are in sharp contrast to our own real feelings, life-long conflicts can arise. We often experience these conflicts as self-disapproval for our own feelings. As a result, such conflicts undermine our happiness and destroy our self-confidence.

For example, if you lost your keys and then said to yourself, "I'm so stupid!", the part of you that tells you you're stupid represents a perfectionistic, critical attitude that has been imposed on you. This attitude may have come to you through a parent or older sibling and later have been reinforced by school, job or spouse. This critical attitude attacks us whenever we make mistakes, which is bound to happen. The Gestalt approach works toward resolving these conflicts in favor of accepting yourself as an individual who can and will make mistakes.

Gestalt-type therapists do not try to unearth instincts or

interpret behavior, nor do they aim to modify behavior in a predetermined direction. The Gestalt approach purports to have you "feel" things out rather than "figure" them out, in order to make you fully aware of your *true* thoughts and feelings—not those you think are expected of you. Gestalt therapists create an environment that helps you to express emotions that you have suppressed in the past and that you are suppressing now; by becoming aware of your emotions you can really "own" them and take satisfaction in expressing your true feelings. This leads to becoming a "whole" person.

Why can't therapists get together and decide the best way to help people? Why are there so many therapies? Is one better than another?

While everyone has an opinion, no one knows for sure that any one therapy is intrinsically better than another. This is because no one has yet been able to measure the results of therapies in an absolute, scientific sense. We can only judge them in terms of how useful they are in a particular set of circumstances involving a particular person and his or her therapist. This is why many therapists use mainly one approach and borrow techniques from other approaches when and where and with whom it will be helpful. This is also why it is important for you to know something about these therapies. If you know something about them, you will be able to consider switching to another form of therapy when you think it will be beneficial to you, even when your therapist does not suggest it.

I have a friend who went through EST and now is trying to talk me—and everyone else he knows—into going through it too. How do you feel about therapies like EST and other groups like this?

Many professionals are very hostile toward these programs. I must admit that I, too, am very critical, although I think that for some people these therapies offer real benefits.

The problem with these programs is their cultlike nature. Practitioners frequently insist that people accept everything they say without doubt or questioning. Instead of being encouraged to see how what has been said can contribute to making a desirable change in their lives, people are pressured and sometimes even coerced to adopt the message and use it as their entire way of life. This creates problems; many people cannot fully accept the message and just abandon it completely, sometimes feeling that they've failed, and sometimes incurring the hostility and condemnation of "believers." Other people—and your friend may be one of these—totally accept the message, in an almost religious way. They eventually become alienated from those who don't go through the program or share their views, which creates other problems.

Another criticism I have of these programs is that they are not individualized—they recommend the same "medicine" for everybody. It's like saying that everyone should have the same diet, which is not true. Depending upon your body type and your own personal leanings, you may or may not benefit from a particular diet. This creates problems when people try to force themselves into the mold that these programs demand, one which may not really be suitable for them.

For some people, however, the content—the actual message—of these programs is very positive, and that I support. Sometimes the people who run these programs are able to create the type of environment in which people do listen to what they have to say, and I have spoken to a large number of patients who have reported very positive results.

TOOLS AND TECHNIQUES

I've been divorced now for seven years and my children are grown. I realize my life is not all it could be and I'd like to try psychotherapy to help me with my problems. But I'm still a little frightened of it and would like to know more about it. How does psychotherapy work? What does the therapist do to help me?

There are many tools and techniques used during the course of the various therapies that are used to promote understanding and change. Most of them are introduced in the therapist's office, though you may be asked to try new things in your daily life, as well. The most commonly used are: reflection and clarification, interpretation, transference, free association, catharsis, dream interpretation, implosion, desensitization, homework, contracts, role-playing, cognitive restructuring, conditioning, "say it again," "let the little child talk," "the empty chair," and hypnosis.

• *Reflection and Clarification*   Your therapist restates what you say in a way that clarifies what you may have had trouble saying or expressing. Sometimes you can get caught up in details, or superficialities, or are simply unable to focus clearly on an issue or feeling.

• *Interpretation*   Your therapist helps you explore hidden or undiscovered meanings and motivations for the things you do. For example, you may wait to mention something important until the end of a therapy session, and the therapist may interpret this as your desire to avoid too much discussion about the subject. A "Freudian slip," where you say something by accident, may also be interpreted as you having inadvertently said what you *really* mean. There's an old story about a patient who once said to Freud, "Can I see you now and play later?" (instead of "pay later"). Freud interpreted this slip to mean that the patient wasn't taking the therapy seriously enough. In another situation, anger toward your boss may be interpreted as unresolved anger toward one or both of your parents.

• *Transference* This occurs to some degree in all therapies, but is particularly fostered and dealt with in the analytic therapies. Transference invokes your transferring to your therapist strong feelings that were originally directed toward other people in your life. Transference is encouraged in the analytic therapy relationship (where an analyst doesn't tell you very much about himself or herself and therefore remains a "blank screen.") So you are able to project onto him or her your own perception of the world. For example, you may think that the therapist is much older than he or she actually is; the therapist may interpret this transference as your need to be a child who is taken care of by an "older" therapist.

Or perhaps you feel that your therapist is not really listening to you. Your perception would lead to a discussion of your conception of the therapist (who it is assumed *is* listening) as it relates to your past experiences of people ignoring you.

• *Free Association* This is another technique that is used primarily by psychoanalytic therapists. During free association, you tell your therapist any thought or feeling that enters your mind, without interruption, and without questioning its meaning, relevance, or acceptability. Through this technique, you are able to see more of your unconscious mind, and so perhaps become closer to the nature and source of your conflicts.

• *Catharsis* This is an analytic term used to describe the relief we feel after we have expressed thoughts and feelings that we have held up inside us. As a result of catharsis, you may have a more uplifted, clearer view of yourself.

• *Dream Interpretation* Psychoanalysts feel that dreams are the most direct indication of what is happening in your unconscious mind. Freud called dreams "the royal road to the unconscious." In psychoanalytic dream interpretation, you and your therapist discover the connection or "association" between your unconscious and the dream it produced. Gestalt therapists may take this one step further, asking you to focus on reliving the dream during the therapy session to help you come to terms with all the emotions that are produced in the dream.

• *Implosion*   This is a behavioral technique used by some therapists to reduce fear by exaggeration and saturation. What happens when you watch a horror movie over and over again? It eventually gets boring. Implosion is a technique that utilizes our own personal horror movies. If you are afraid of flying, for example, your therapist may ask you to imagine that you are on a plane and that it is crashing. As you can guess, this can be a very intense, draining experience, but eventually these scenes will seem less scary and you will be less afraid to go on a real plane.

• *Desensitization*   This behavioral technique is usually used to reduce fear by pairing it with relaxation. You are trained in a relaxation technique and then gradually introduced to fearful stimuli while remaining in a relaxed state. The relaxation overcomes the fear gradually until you are no longer afraid.

• *Homework*   Homework is a term usually applied by behavioral therapists to describe whatever they expect of you between sessions. Homework generally applies to a specific action that you and your therapist decide you should try during that week. If you are a very shy person, your homework might be going up to five people and asking them for the time of day. If you are claustrophobic, it might involve making some small progress, such as taking a short elevator ride or just standing in an elevator with the door open for a minute. To get more in touch with your feelings, you might be asked to focus on what you are thinking about yourself while talking to your mother on the phone.

Some therapists don't prescribe homework that is this specific. A psychoanalyst might ask you to try to remember your dreams and write them down so you can bring them to the next session. A Gestalt therapist might ask you to try to focus on a feeling you experienced during the session and re-experience it outside the session.

• *Contracts* You make an agreement with the therapist to act in a certain way—to try out a new behavior or to restrain yourself from doing something—usually outside the session. It is really a contract with yourself, and you may be asked to agree to certain rewards when you fulfill the contract (or, sometimes, certain punishments when you do not). The rewards usually involve treating yourself in some positive manner that you wouldn't ordinarily.

You might take a taxi instead of the bus, for example. At any rate, the reward should never be in discordance with your agreement with your therapist. If you are trying to lose weight, for example, and you lose five pounds, you might reward yourself by treating yourself to a new pair of pants—but not an ice cream cone!

• *Role-Playing* This tool is often used in behavioral therapy and sometimes in Gestalt. In behavioral therapy, you and the therapist (or other members of the group, in group therapy) act out certain real-life situations or fantasies. By experiencing a situation in practice, you discover what is difficult about it for you. Your therapist might then guide you toward developing your most effective role. Once you become comfortable playing your part, you can, theoretically, transfer this over to real life. In Gestalt, role-playing allows you to get in touch with your own suppressed feelings, as well as to empathize with those of the other people involved.

• *Cognitive Restructuring* We have certain "preconscious" thoughts, or cognitions, lying just below the surface, of which we are barely aware, if at all. We take these automatic, or assumptive, thoughts so much for granted that we don't realize how irrelevant, inaccurate, or destructive they are. Cognitive restructuring helps you to recognize these thoughts, challenge them, and replace them with other thoughts. For example, when you feel down on yourself after making an obvious mistake, you have a cognition that you *shouldn't* make mistakes, and that if you do, you are a less valuable, competent, worthwhile person. By challenging these irrational thoughts, we are less victimized by them.

• *Conditioning*   Conditioning is a way of thinking about the way we learn. It is easy to understand the simplest form of conditioning if we think of the way we train animals. If Fido does something we want him to do—like come when he is called—we give Fido a reward in order to increase the probability that he will come again when called. If Fido does something we don't want him to do—like tear up our slippers—we punish him in the hope of teaching him not to do it again. We have also learned from watching animals that we can pair certain things in their minds. When you take out Fido's leash, he quickly jumps up, wagging his tail, knowing that he is about to be taken for a walk. This is an example of "classical conditioning."

Behavioral therapists believe that to a *certain extent* our behavior is conditioned. In other words, sometimes the way we act or feel or think is related to the fact that certain types of behavior, feelings and thoughts are encouraged or discouraged by either part or all of our society or culture.

Behavioral therapists point to the following phenomena to illustrate this point: (1) Pavlovian conditioning. We associate something with something else and so attach to this something the value that is applied to the something else. For example, in our society, money is associated with having a comfortable life and with power. As a result, money, the means to this desired or valued end, becomes an end in itself, or an object of value. (2) Skinner's conclusion that certain types of behavior, thoughts and feelings are either rewarded or punished by members of part or all of our society. For example, doing well in school is often rewarded by parents either materially or emotionally. As a result, some children will try to do well in school to receive from their parents high praise or an increase in their weekly allowance.

In therapy, behaviorists use conditioning techniques to help people relearn new behaviors which will be more helpful than the old ones. You should remember, however, that very few therapists use conditioning exclusively.

• *"Say It Again"*   This Gestalt approach aims to help you

get in touch with the emotions that lay under the things that you are saying. For example, you may be describing to the therapist, in a relatively cool, detached way, the fact that your parents forgot your birthday. The therapist may ask you to repeat the phrase "They forgot my birthday" three or four times out loud. This has the effect of bringing to the surface your underlying feelings of hurt and neglect.

• *"Let the Little Child Talk"* This Gestalt technique is based on the notion that somewhere in ourselves the child that we were many years ago still lives. The therapist asks you to mentally contact that child in you and to speak from that part of you. This exercise sometimes helps you to understand where some of your feelings and behaviors are coming from.

• *"The Empty Chair"* This technique is used frequently in Gestalt therapy. You are asked to move back and forth between two different chairs. As you do, you create a dialogue between different parts of yourself, airing different sides of a conflict you are having with yourself or another person. This helps you clarify your thoughts, reach reasonable compromises, and understand more about how others are affecting you.

• *Hypnosis* Hypnosis is variously seen as a different state of consciousness (as are daydreaming, dreaming, and meditation), and as a role of submission to the hypnotist's suggestions. It is traditionally used to break habits such as smoking or overeating by direct suggestion or aversion therapy. It may also be used to get around certain memory blocks that come up in more general psychotherapy by getting you to relax and feel more open.

I've been hearing a lot about biofeedback. Is this used in psychotherapy?

Biofeedback is a relatively new technique commonly used by psychotherapists to treat the following problems: tension headaches, insomnia, and phobias. Biofeedback can also be used as a general relaxation technique. The patient is hooked up to a biofeedback machine which monitors one or more biological functions—usually skin temperature or muscle tension. These "autonomous" functions are the body's way of showing inner tension and were previously thought to be involuntary (unable to be controlled consciously). But by paying attention to the information (feedback in the form of a light or a sound) that the biofeedback machine registers, the patient learns to control these functions, and as a result, his or her tension.

I'm very much against using drugs to solve problems. I think it's a cop-out. Why are drugs sometimes used in psychotherapy? Do they really cure anything?

Drugs can have an effect on our brains and subsequently our thoughts and feelings, so they are sometimes used in an attempt to treat emotional problems. These "psychotropic" drugs fall into four main groups: Minor tranquilizers such as Valium; antidepressants or mood elevators such as Elavil; sedative-hypnotics such as phenobarbitol and other barbiturates; and antipsychotics such as Thorazine. Drugs do not, in general, cure or attack the cause of our problems; they offer only temporary relief of certain symptoms. In addition, they can have serious side effects. Therefore, some form of psychotherapy is usually given along with these drugs.

I recently saw a TV show where people were dancing and drawing as means of therapy. They called this form of therapy "expressive." How do expressive techniques help people solve their mental problems?

Expressive techniques include a wide range of therapeutic techniques such as art therapy, music therapy, dance therapy, and for children, play therapy. These activities help people express emotions that they are not able to express verbally and so achieve a sense of release and well-being. These techniques may also provide material for interpretation, much the way dreams do, and as a result, psychotherapists often prescribe these techniques for their patients.

FORMS OF PSYCHOTHERAPY

I have problems, my husband and I have problems, and my whole family has problems. Can you explain the advantages and disadvantages of going to a therapist alone, as a couple, as a family, or entering a group?

Individual therapy is the most common approach. Just as an individual goes to a medical doctor for physical problems, the thinking here is that since *you* are the one having the problem, *you* go to the expert for help. The advantage of individual therapy is that you and the therapist are able to focus intensely on your problems for the entire time of the session. This form of treatment gives you the opportunity to be most expressive without being concerned about the reactions of other people (except for the therapist, of course).

Couples therapy can be advantageous, especially when your problems exist primarily between you and your husband. The therapist gets to *see,* firsthand, both sides of the story. Contrast this with individual therapy, where the therapist has to rely on the reports of one person, and you can understand why couples therapy is sometimes the better approach. However, you will find that couples therapy is very confrontational. This can be a disadvantage when the people involved are too angry, defensive, or antagonistic toward each other to see how their own actions might possibly be contributing to their shared conflict. In this case, it is usually better to treat each person individually, or to treat each person as part of a couple *and* individually.

Family therapy usually involves most or all members of the immediate family, and sometimes members of the extended family. The idea here is that problems originate in the family and can be resolved in the family. The family is a social unit and can be a strong vehicle for social change. If you choose family therapy, the therapist will try to act as a catalyst to improve the way your family works together. One of the great advantages of family therapy is that it doesn't stigmatize any one member of the family as being "the patient." On the minus side, the contact with the therapist can be less intense, and sometimes people are unwilling to talk about certain issues in front of their children or parents.

Group therapy was developed originally because it had the advantage of being much more economical than individual therapy. As group therapy has evolved, it has become apparent that there are advantages that have nothing to do with money. Groups allow you to get more than one person's feedback; people get to actually see you interact with others, rather than your just reporting it as you would in individual therapy. This live-action has the advantage of revealing problems that you might not otherwise bring up to the therapist, either because you are unaware of them, or because you don't want to face them. The disadvantages include the possibility of getting "lost" in the group (you have to fight for time). Thus, sometimes it may not be as economical for the patient as it seems. The group may also go astray; all that feedback from so many sources may be confusing to you.

SPECIALIZED APPROACHES

Everything has gotten so specialized these days. Has psychotherapy begun to specialize in the way medicine has?

Yes; in recent years, psychotherapists have also begun to specialize in treating specific types of problems. The most common areas of specialization are in sex therapy, alcohol and drug problems, eating disorders, phobias, and stress reduction.

The advantage of this approach is that your therapist will probably be very interested in and have great expertise in his or her chosen area of specialization. Another plus is that it fosters the formation of therapy groups consisting of people who share similar problems. This helps remove any stigma or alienation that may be attached to your problem; in addition, one member's success can spur similar improvement in others in the group.

The disadvantage of specialization is that such therapy may focus only on the one problem and treat it from that single, narrow point of view. In so doing, it may overlook other problems the person may be having, including those that may be contributing to the presenting symptom. For example, a man may see a sex therapist because of impotence. If the root of his problem is really a general lack of confidence, it might be more helpful for him to have assertiveness training or another, more broadly focused therapy before the sexual problem is dealt with at all.

CHAPTER THREE

Who Does Psychotherapy and Where

WHO DOES PSYCHOTHERAPY

I've been seeing lots of ads in magazines and newspapers for psychotherapy. What is the difference between one psychotherapist and another?

Psychotherapists can vary greatly from one to another, and it is difficult—and sometimes impossible—to tell from an advertisement whether any one in particular is qualified. Unfortunately for the general public, the title "psychotherapist" is not generally regulated by law. Legally, anyone—regardless of education or experience—can call himself or herself a psychotherapist. However, a large number of professional people such as psychiatrists, psychologists, social workers, nurses, and ministers are specially trained in the practice of psychotherapy. These titles *are* regulated and the professionals to whom they belong have either a license or certification to practice. In general, I believe it is best to avoid psychotherapy with those who are not in a licensed profession.

I know that lots of different doctors and non-doctors do psychotherapy. Who are the different professionals who are trained to do psychotherapy?

Most psychotherapists are either psychiatrists, psychologists, social workers, or nurse-clinicians.

• *Psychiatrist* Psychiatrists are physicians who have gone through medical school, a hospital internship, and usually a three-year residency in psychiatry. They then take an exam which, if passed, makes them board-certified psychiatrists. Since they are physicians, psychiatrists are aware of the medical aspects of psychological problems, and they are able to prescribe drugs. In addition, they may have hospital-admitting privileges, which is helpful in case hospitalization is needed.

• *Psychologist* Psychologists are professionals who have been either licensed or certified by the governing board of the state in which they practice. The regulations vary from state to state as to education and experience required. In most states, licensed psychologists have either a Ph.D., Psy.D., or Ed.D.; they have had supervised clinical training and experience; and they have passed an examination.

Psychologists do not have formal training in medicine; rather, they have concentrated their studies on the psychology of human development and behavior.

• *Social Worker* The requirements for the licensing of social workers also vary from state to state. It usually requires at least a Master's Degree in Social Work and passing the state licensing exam; some states also require two or three additional years of experience and specialized training. Social workers practice therapy in a wide variety of situations, using many different psychological and psychosocial techniques which emphasize the interaction between people and various aspects of the society in which we live.

• *Nurse-Clinician* A nurse-clinician is also called a psychiatric nurse and is a licensed practical nurse or registered nurse. He or she also has had special training in the field of mental health, often leading to a Master of Science degree in psychiatric nursing. This therapist has a medical background, and so is particularly aware of the medical aspects of psychiatric disorders. Sometimes nurse-clinicians specialize in treating the psychological ramifications of people who have medical disorders.

My sister, who is an alcoholic, went for group therapy to a clinic. She says she was helped, even though the group was conducted by someone without a degree in psychotherapy—just an ordinary person who was an ex-alcoholic. Is it possible she's right? Can non-professionals help?

Yes, paraprofessionals such as the one who led your sister's group can often be quite helpful. Most have received their expertise either in short training programs or on the job, although some have undergraduate work or two-year degrees in psychology. Paraprofessionals may also be called mental health workers, community workers, street workers, or volunteers. Paraprofessionals are usually not licensed, but they generally practice under the supervision of professionals, either in an institution such as a hospital, a clinic, or in private practice.

Sometimes paraprofessionals are ex-patients, i.e., ex-addicts, ex-alcoholics, ex-phobics. Although these ex-sufferer paraprofessionals may be lacking in formalized training compared with professionals, their own experience gives them the advantage of being better able to understand and of being better equipped to help someone else who is in a similar situation.

Some time ago I was having troubles with my marriage and I didn't know where else to turn, so I spoke with my minister. I was surprised to learn that he had actually had some training in psychotherapy. Is this usual? Why doesn't everyone just talk with their minister when they have problems?

It is often the case that pastoral counselors—nuns, priests, ministers, and rabbis who have had some mental health training—also offer psychotherapy. Many people such as yourself may prefer a pastoral counselor because they already know the person and may feel more comfortable because of their similar religious point of view, particularly if the therapeutic issue involves religion or morality. For others, however, the pastoral counselor's religious orientation may prove too narrow.

37

WHERE THEY PRACTICE

I live in a big city and there are so many places that offer psychotherapy that I'm having trouble deciding which one to go to. Where is the best place to go for psychotherapy? How important is the setting in which psychotherapy is practiced?

As you have discovered, psychotherapy is practiced in a wide range of settings: private practice, group practice, outpatient clinic, community mental health center, and hospital clinic. The setting is somewhat important because its various characteristics may affect your attitude and the therapist's reaction and responsibility to you. I believe, however, that excellent therapy can take place in almost any setting. (The setting will also affect the fee.)

I'm a very private person and I think I would prefer going to a psychotherapist in private practice. Am I right that this would be best for me? What are the other advantages and disadvantages of therapy in this type of setting?

A therapist in private practice works alone in his or her own office. You have already hit upon the primary advantage of this—privacy: There are fewer people to run into in the waiting room and your records are seen only by your therapist. In addition, you control the choice of the individual therapist and are able to negotiate the terms of the therapy (day, hour, fee, etc.). Another plus lies in the fact that the therapist depends upon you to provide the fee—and this may be an incentive for the therapist to invest more during the session. It may, however, influence the course of your therapy in a way detrimental to your interests—your therapy may be less confrontational and/or it may continue longer than it otherwise might because the therapist is reluctant to lose you as a patient. Another disadvantage is that you see only one therapist—and that person may not be the best for you. The fee is quite likely to be higher, since therapists in private practice have completed their training and are experienced professionals.

How does group practice differ from private practice?

A group practice usually is made up of a number of therapists who have gotten together to share offices and services. Group practice is essentially the same as private practice, except there is cross-fertilization and sharing of referrals, which may be to your advantage. You may lose somewhat in confidentiality, since other people may have access to your records and your therapist will probably discuss your case with the other members of the practice. You may have slightly less choice in picking a therapist because the group may assign one of their members to you.

I've looked into it and I've found an outpatient clinic, a community mental health center, and a hospital clinic near me. What are the differences between them?

They may seem very similar to you, but they do differ. Free-standing outpatient clinics are usually state-licensed and independent of any institution; community mental health centers are large institutions devoted solely to treating psychiatric disorders; hospital clinics are run by the hospitals' departments of psychiatry.

What these settings do have in common is a full range of professionals practicing psychotherapy, with much cross-fertilization of minds. Also, they rarely send you elsewhere for any additional psychiatric service. They often get some public funding, so the fees are generally lower than those in either private or group practice settings.

However, in all three, confidentiality may suffer, and it's possible that you will be assigned a therapist-in-training (who may be a psychology intern, a psychiatric resident, or a social work student, albeit a supervised one). You may be transferred to another therapist, since the staff is less stable than in private practice. Therapists in these three settings draw a salary—a disadvantage in that they are paid whether you are satisfied or not, an advantage in that they can remain totally true to what they feel is the best therapy without fear of losing income. Though similar in many ways to hospital clinics, freestanding clinics do not provide hospitalization services.

Community health centers and hospital clinics have an additional advantage in that you are assured that there is someone who is available 24 hours a day to handle emergency phone calls and who also has access to your records. If you have therapy in the other settings—private and group practice and many freestanding clinics—there may not be anyone on 24-hour call and you must be content with contacting the emergency room of a local hospital during a crisis. Finally, the psychiatric department in a hospital will also be able to provide hospitalization if necessary, unlike the other settings, which will, however, be able to refer you to a hospital.

CHAPTER FOUR

Choosing a Psychotherapist

WHERE TO FIND A PSYCHOTHERAPIST

After looking into it, I've decided that psychotherapy is for me. But how do I begin to choose a good psychotherapist?

First you have to find a few from whom to make your choice. Luckily, there are many sources for names and recommendations.

• *Referral agencies or the local societies of the various professions.* This is one place to begin. Examples are the state psychological association, the state psychiatric association, the county medical association or social work association. They may send you a directory with names and addresses of therapists in your area and possibly also their affiliations. Admittedly, this is not very much information to go on, but at least it's a place to start. If you are interested in a particular type of orientation—Gestalt, for instance—you can look for the organizations to which this type of therapist belongs.

• *Your family practitioner.* Another frequent source of psychotherapists is the family practitioner. He or she will usually be able to refer you to a therapist. You can also speak to your clergyman, who may know a therapist or who may have training in psychotherapy himself.

• *The phone book.* You can look in the yellow pages of your phone book under the headings of psychotherapist, psychiatrist, psychologist, social worker, or under some special heading such as family therapy, marriage therapy, alcoholism, drug abuse, and so on. You may also call the places in which therapy is practiced—hospitals, mental health centers, outpatient clinics, and special services—which are discussed in Chapter Three. Although some professionals cast a disapproving eye upon psychotherapists who advertise, newspaper ads are another potential source.

Unless you live in a very small town or rural area, finding a therapist is really not that big a problem. Finding the right one for *you* is the hard part.

My brother has been going to a therapist that he swears by and has recommended her to me. Are friends and relatives good sources for recommendations?

You can certainly ask your friends and relatives. A lot of referrals in psychotherapy are by word of mouth, and this has its positive and negative aspects. On the positive side, you're really getting other people's reports which are more helpful than just a listing of names and titles and credentials. On the other hand, sometimes people feel obligated to like the therapist that someone has referred them to. So if you go this route, make it clear to your brother that you are going to be choosing from among a number of therapists.

After I get the list of psychotherapists, should I have therapy with the first therapist I like, or should I shop around?

It's always better to shop around, but this is especially so if you are new to psychotherapy. You should commit yourself to one session with each of two or three people. You need to get a feeling for what different therapists are like so you have some basis for comparison. If you've never been to a therapist, there's no other way you can judge.

What? Even if I like the first therapist, I should waste money on two other sessions?

It may seem that way to you now, but it's really not a waste of money. The chances are you will be overwhelmingly tempted to like the first therapist you see and cancel any others. But because therapy is generally a long-term process, it's worth investing the extra money at the beginning rather than diving into therapy with the first person you see. The cost of the two extra sessions is minimal compared with the total sum that you will spend on therapy.

MAKING THE CHOICE

After I've seen a few therapists, how do I know which one is the right one for me?

There are basically four factors to consider when choosing a therapist: qualifications (training and experience); orientation (type of therapy practiced); setting; and personal preferences.

1. *Qualifications* Check his or her credentials—a license or certification should be displayed on the wall of the office. If not, don't be afraid to ask. The therapist will not be offended; if anything, your checking shows a qualified therapist that you recognize and appreciate that background and training are important. You might also ask whether the therapist has had experience treating people with your particular difficulties.

2. *Orientation* This is one of the most difficult factors to evaluate. To choose well, you need to have some familiarity with the basic theories and practices in the field of psychotherapy (see Chapter Two). Ask the therapist to explain the orientation he or she favors and how it will work in your case. Or will a combination of approaches work best? How will the therapist interact with you during therapy? Try to get at least a ballpark figure as to how long the therapy will take.

3. *Setting* To evaluate this factor, turn to Chapter Three for the pros and cons of each; then judge for yourself firsthand by visiting those which sound right for you.

4. *Personal Preferences* These include age, gender, man-

ner, and racial, sexual, religious, or class prejudice. You should take all of them into consideration because a therapist who satisfies your preferences will help make you more comfortable throughout the therapy. For example, there are dramatic differences in manner and style, even among those who call themselves psychoanalysts. A warm, friendly, supportive, relaxed person might put you more at ease than one who is cool, detached, thoughtful, restrained and unresponsive. On the other hand, a too warm and friendly person may lead you to feel you have to please that person or make it more difficult to express anger which usually comes up somewhere during the therapy.

What about fees? How much can I expect to pay for therapy?

The therapist usually volunteers this information; if not, ask what the usual fee is, whether it is negotiable, and the preferred method or schedule of payment. The amount you pay is not necessarily directly related to the quality of the therapy—geographical area plays a big part, and so does the amount of experience. Even how well his or her practice is going can play a part. Therapists in private practice in big cities are getting up to $100 per session, but high quality therapy can be found for $35 to $50, or less. Outpatient clinics usually charge less than private therapists, or have sliding scales.

As far as fees are concerned, I generally recommend that you don't box yourself in. If you have only $1,000 to spend on therapy, don't go to someone who charges $100 a visit—that limits you to ten sessions. It is better to go to someone who charges $45 a visit because that will give you more leeway. Remember, though, that psychotherapy may be at least partly covered by your health insurance policy. So check it out thoroughly before you begin; each session might be costing you only $10 instead of $50.

What other questions should I ask the therapist? How much of this information can I get over the phone?

You can do a lot of your initial screening over the phone, but therapists generally do not like to spend more than five or ten minutes on this, so be prepared and get to the point.

First, you can ask about fees and credentials. The therapist should also be willing to spend a few minutes on the phone to tell you about availability—how often and at what time of day can that person be seen, is he or she available on weekends or evenings, for extra sessions, and can you call at other times if you have a crisis or emergency?

You might ask if the individual treats people with your particular problem, and to briefly describe his or her orientation. However, for a thorough discussion of orientation and length of therapy, and to judge personal preferences, you must schedule a session with the therapist. Only during a bona fide session can you interview and get to know a therapist as if you were hiring someone for a job, which is in part what you are doing.

I've seen a couple of therapists on a first-session basis, and they seem qualified. How do I actually decide which therapist to go with?

Therapists are not just experts, they are people with their own quirks and personalities. Sometimes individuals just "click" with each other; sometimes they don't. After you have contrasted and compared all the factors listed above, you must ultimately ask yourself: Which person do I like best? Whom do I most trust and have faith in? With whom am I most comfortable?

So far, no studies have shown conclusively that one method, technique, or school of psychotherapy works better than any other. Of course it is important to be sure you are going to a qualified professional for your own safety, but many people feel that your own positive feelings and expectations are more critical than specific credentials in determining the successful outcome of the therapy.

CHAPTER FIVE

Making the Most of Psychotherapy

BEGINNING THERAPY

I've never had therapy before and I'm nervous about what to expect. How does therapy begin? What are the first sessions like?

It's easy to understand why you may be somewhat nervous and uneasy about confiding in a stranger for the first time and about looking at yourself critically. Many people feel unsure of themselves and the therapist. Others, however, experience some immediate sense of relief once they have made the decision to begin therapy.

When you begin therapy, bear in mind that your first few sessions with the therapist will probably be unlike those that follow. Your therapist will be asking a lot of questions at this point in order to find out as much as possible about you. He or she will begin the therapy by asking, for example, why you are in therapy, and why you believe you need treatment.

In addition, your therapist will ask you both relevant and seemingly irrelevant questions as he or she tries to go below the surface to find out what is really causing your problems. So don't be surprised if you have come to therapy because you fight with your husband and the therapist asks you to talk about your mother. Your therapist may believe that some of the problems you are having with your husband actually have to do with your childhood relationship with your mother.

Your first sessions will also differ from later sessions in that you may get less interaction and feedback than you will later on. Your therapist may not say very much—particularly if the orientation is psychoanalytic—and this may throw you off and make you feel lost. If your therapist seems unresponsive, this is because he or she may not want to shape the session, to restrict what is going to happen. You shouldn't be discouraged by this; just ask the therapist how typical it is, and what you can expect the therapy to be like in the future.

I'm not much of a talker, and it's particularly embarrassing to talk about myself honestly. I wonder: How does the therapist get me to talk?

This varies greatly according to the orientation and personality of the therapist. Take heart in the fact that you are not alone: Many people are reluctant to enter therapy because of this problem. Analytic therapists usually will wait you out: They will ask a few questions, but mostly they sit there and wait for you to begin talking. Most people find the silence so unbearable that they do eventually begin to talk. Other therapists may give you a direction to follow during a session and provide more of a structure by asking questions or by assigning you certain exercises as explained in Chapter Two.

Though it may be difficult at first, you will soon find it easier and easier to tell your therapist even your deepest, most embarrassing secrets. If you are like most people, you are aware of constantly being judged by other people, even on a subtle level. It's different in therapy. Almost all therapists try to remain nonjudgmental, thus creating an atmosphere that is unique in their patients' experience. Gradually, you adjust to and absorb the new, freer climate characteristic of psychotherapy that allows you to open up more than you are used to, since what often prevents people from talking is a fear of being judged. You can say *anything* to a therapist and you will not be judged, and this attitude is the most important "tool" in the therapist's repertoire.

RIGHTS AND RESPONSIBILITIES

What do I have the right to expect from the therapist?

Unlike a friendship, the relationship between you and your therapist is structured. Each person has certain responsibilities and rights. You should consider each other as social equals, and treat each other with mutual respect. You can expect the therapist to be a catalyst, to apply his or her expertise to help you in the process of change you are looking for. To that end, the therapist should pay attention to you and provide the nonjudgmental environment mentioned earlier.

In addition, your therapist should show professional discretion and refrain from abusing any power he or she has over you, or from taking advantage of your vulnerability. Although not all therapists are warm and responsive, he or she should give you helpful feedback in some form—in analysis it might be an interpretation, in Gestalt it might be an emotive exercise, in behaviorism it might be a homework assignment. You should also be assured of confidentiality within the limits of the practice and setting, and of having access to your records if you wish.

What will the therapist expect from me?

Basically, your therapist expects you to be truthful and to come into therapy with a serious attitude. Your therapist must feel that you are there in order to truly attempt some kind of change. It is frustrating for us to treat people who enter therapy solely to please someone else or because someone has badgered them into it. You should enter therapy with an open mind—the narrower your attitude, the more limited the potential of the therapy. So try to remain receptive to hearing things you did not expect to hear.

In addition, the therapist expects you to come on time for appointed sessions, to present material for therapy, and to pay the mutually agreed-upon fee.

EVALUATING PROGRESS

I'm a rather impatient person. I don't want to wait forever to get better. When can I expect to see results? I know someone who's been in therapy for years—will it take that long for me?

This question is asked by almost every patient I see for the first time. Unfortunately, I usually can't give a clear-cut answer. The length of therapy varies tremendously, not only with the orientation and expectancy of the therapist, but with the individual and the severity of the problem. I once had a patient who had been in a car accident and as a result had developed a fear of driving. I was able to treat her successfully in seven sessions. Most problems, however, are deep-seated and take much longer. Serious or incapacitating problems such as depression or compulsions should not be approached with quick solutions or easy answers, no matter how much they appeal to you as an impatient person.

The length of therapy also varies with what you mean by results. In some therapies—particularly behavioral and Gestalt—the therapist expects at least small changes in a relatively short period of time. In more analytic therapies, these changes are not expected for a much longer period of time. In general, analytic therapies tend to be more extended, to require more visits per week—although there are shorter versions of analytic therapy also. In the other two major forms, sometimes people are seen very successfully over a period of months.

Sometimes patients come in with deceptively modest problems. A man came to see me because he was being called upon to speak in front of a work group and he usually had trouble with public speaking. Therapy revealed that he was very ashamed of a great many things in his life. We opened up the scope of the therapy and he became a much longer-term patient than we had at first imagined.

Why can therapy take so long?

Therapy seems to take a long time because, even when people say they want to change, they are still somewhat resistant to it. There are several reasons for this.

• *Fear of the Unknown* We humans in general are terribly afraid of things we do not know. No matter how miserable we are, at least we are familiar—and, in a way, comfortable—with our misery.

• *Defense Against Pain* Another hitch in the process of change occurs because our psychological problems usually arise from situations in which we once felt afraid, or ashamed, or guilty. Therapy sometimes involves revealing and reliving these old sufferings, and therefore poses the possibility of again feeling the pain. We have all developed many defenses against these negative feelings which save us the pain but make changing difficult.

• *Change Takes Time.* Finally, it has taken us many years to learn to be just the way we are. We are not the infuriatingly rational Mr. Spock, nor computers whose programs can be changed with a flick of the wrist and a push of the button. As humans, we have to go through a long slow process of relearning, reconditioning, reunderstanding and reexamining.

So, you see there are many factors operating against us in therapy. It is not easy to change the way we are. On the other hand, we can probably expect some change, even if small, before a great amount of time has passed.

A friend of mine has been going to therapy and he says he's satisfied with the way things are going. I don't notice any change in him, though. If I do have therapy, how will I know whether the therapy is working?

You will know that the therapy is working if you are getting at least some of what you want to get out of it. But be forewarned: You may not necessarily feel better at first—in fact you may feel worse!

It is important that you understand what the goals of the therapy are, what to expect. This is the only way you have of knowing where you are at any given point in the therapy. Say, for example, that you are being treated by a psychoanalyst. You and your therapist have come to an agreement that understanding the connections you made in your childhood would help you in your present life. Even though the symptoms you are experiencing may remain the same, the therapy should help you understand at least some of what went on in your childhood. If the goals are concrete and clear-cut, as they are with the behavioral treatment of sexual problems or phobias, you should expect to see some small, and perhaps great, symptom relief as the therapy goes on.

What should I do if I'm not sure? I'm afraid I can't be objective. Can't I just trust the therapist?

It's important to walk the fine line between trusting that the therapy is having or will have benefit, and being wary that not enough is happening. When you feel that you are not getting results, it is important to discuss this with your therapist, and to make this part of the therapy.

Don't make the mistake of keeping your doubts to yourself. People often feel that this is something that they can't discuss with the therapist—that it is too threatening to the therapist, that he or she will get angry at them. Instead of being open and candid, they sometimes get fed up and leave abruptly. Any doubts you have should be an ongoing issue; the therapist may tell you that your doubts are part of your problem and that you're ignoring the progress that's being made, or that you're impatient. Of course, this may or may not be true—ultimately you have to be the judge and decide where trust ends and whether you're getting what you're looking for.

If you have a pattern of impatience in your life, of a lack of commitment, of being unable to stick with something, I think you should be suspicious of your discontent. If you are not a particularly impatient person, and you have a definite and clear feeling that the therapy is not moving along fast enough, you should continue to bring up the topic with your therapist. If the two of you are unable to resolve it, I recommend that you switch to another therapist.

My mother and father say they liked me better before I started therapy; I get the impression from my friends that they're not too pleased about it either. Should I listen to my family or friends when they tell me their opinions about how effective the therapy is?

Generally, no. Friends and family are hardly the best judges—chances are they either have some stake in your staying the way you are or they may be overly eager to see you change in some way that pleases them. Therapy is probably the most personal thing a person can do, and that makes you the best judge of the way it's progressing. Of course, it might be wise to listen and to try to objectively evaluate what others say. But don't ever give the responsibility for the evaluation of the therapy over to anybody else.

COMMON PROBLEMS WITH THERAPY

All my friends and most of my family are pleased that I've decided to have psychotherapy. But I'm secretly afraid they won't like the new me. How will my friends and family react if I do change?

Many times family and friends have told us that we need the therapy in the first place, and they may be very enthusiastic about it. On the other hand, we must realize that even the most supportive, enthusiastic people have gotten used to us the way we have been. So, in spite of what people may say, you should expect some resistance to your changing. Also, when people recommend we go into therapy, they often have some specific change in mind. But this may not be the direction in which you actually change once the therapy has started.

Take, for example, the man who was berated by his wife. Day in and day out she said to him, "Be a man." When this man went into therapy and became more assertive, the wife found she didn't like the man he became. Now she has no one to berate—when she tries to berate him, he doesn't react the way he used to, and he sometimes gets angry. Maybe the wife didn't really want her husband to be a man after all; what she really wanted was to have someone around that she could *tell* to be a man.

There is often a rough period for both the patient and the people around him or her during the changing process. You may act and feel worse as old conflicts and pains are exposed and relived through. This naturally produces some difficulties in your relationships with others, and they may need to learn to increase their tolerance of your moods and needs. But when the dust settles, people usually adjust and the relationships are better than they were originally. However, in some cases—where serious difficulties cannot be resolved— the relationships do break up. You should understand that and take the potential hazard into consideration before you begin therapy.

I've heard all these stories about women falling in love with their therapists. What happens if I feel I'm becoming too dependent upon my therapist—or falling in love with him?

This is a common question. People sometimes fear this will happen, and sometimes it does happen. The answer is a fairly simple one: Talk to your therapist about it. In many therapies it is considered natural to become somewhat attached, and even attracted, to the therapist during the course of the therapy. If the person is helping you, naturally you're going to be dependent on him. However, you should find that as the therapy draws closer to a successful conclusion and you are able to accomplish what you want to on your own, these feelings will subside. Falling in love with your therapist frequently is tied up with your fantasies, and usually grows out of the process of transference we talked about in Chapter Two. In analytic thinking, it is considered part of the treatment and a good prognostic sign.

I've been hearing about therapists seducing their patients. What should I do if my therapist suggests that we become intimate sexually?

It is clear that these seductions have occurred—some cases having been highly publicized—but their actual numbers may have been exaggerated. This type of behavior is totally disapproved of by all the professions practicing psychotherapy. If such a proposition is made by your therapist, you should terminate the therapy and report the incident to the licensing organization of that person's profession. This is not only for your own protection, but also out of concern for possible future patients who may also be subjected to this type of behavior.

What do I do if my therapist goes away, or if I have an emergency?

Patients usually do without therapy during their therapists' vacations; in fact, patients occasionally time their own vacations to coincide with their therapists'. However, you should not feel abandoned and alone while your therapist is away; most vacationing therapists arrange to have some other therapist "cover" their practice. This means that in an emergency you can call and schedule visits with someone who may have access to your records and who may have been briefed about your situation by your therapist. If your therapist has not made such arrangements, or if you have an emergency during which you cannot get in touch with your therapist, you can always go to the emergency room of the local general hospital. A psychiatric resident should be on duty, or someone who can provide emergency service for you.

CHANGING THERAPISTS

I've been in therapy for several months and I'm really not satisfied with the way things are going. I've thought about changing therapists and even talked about it, but I still haven't been able to make the move. Why is it so difficult to change therapists?

There are usually two difficulties here. The first lies in actually reaching that decision and being certain that you do want to see someone else. Sometimes the idea of changing therapists involves running away from the therapy rather than making a productive change. The second involves feeling a sense of loss because no matter how badly the therapy has gone, you have probably forged some sort of bond with the therapist. Some people find it very difficult to separate, no matter how advisable it may be. If you have discussed your decision to change with the therapist, he or she may agree and be happy to refer you to another. Sometimes the therapist may disagree and insist you are running away. But remember, you are the only one who can judge this, ultimately.

ENDING THERAPY

I think I'm ready to end therapy, but my therapist hasn't mentioned it. Who decides when it's time to end the therapy?

Although ending therapy is ultimately in your control, this is really a decision that you and your therapist should reach together. Your thoughts about ending therapy are part of the therapy, and you should not keep them to yourself. Always discuss these thoughts with your therapist. Your therapist may not have mentioned ending therapy because most likely you may think the therapy is finished sooner than the therapist. Your therapist probably has wider goals and feels you could progress further or may be aware of your desire to terminate at a particularly difficult point. With some shorter-term therapies, however, the reverse is true: The therapist "pushes you out into the world" to show you how well you can do without him or her.

Alternatively, you may want to consider taking just a break from therapy and this is also something to discuss. Sometimes your therapist may bring up the possibility of your terminating, or your changing therapists or modalities, such as from individual to group, or your trying activities other than therapy for a while.

If your therapist disagrees with you, it is his or her job to help you clarify the need you feel, but not to coerce you into staying. If you can't eventually agree with your therapist, consult another one.

But how do I know when it's time to stop?

The end of your relationship with your therapist may be exciting and satisfying—you both may know when it's right to stop. Sometimes, however, it is filled with doubt and ambivalence. Some people are afraid of stopping, of leaving the support of therapy. Termination is easiest when you have set up a specific goal or goals. If you have achieved those goals, it's time to end the therapy.

In general, you can look for these signs: feeling a sense of mastery and strength, of the ability to solve your own problems, of the acceptance that therapy cannot provide the solutions to all your problems or make you a perfect human being. Perhaps therapy has even become boring!

How do I do it—do I just break off cold turkey, or is it best to taper off gradually?

This too is best answered through a discussion with your therapist. Many therapists, myself included, believe that a tapering-off process is advisable in most cases. Usually this is a gradual, short-term tapering off—from once a week to every other week, to once a month, and then stopping. I don't believe in extending this tapering off over a long period of time because it is by no means fatal to stop—you can always initiate therapy again. Remember: Stopping therapy is not dangerous in the vast majority of cases. It can be a mistake, but if you can keep an open mind, it's a mistake that can be corrected.

I'm afraid that the results of therapy won't last. What happens after I've been off therapy for a while and feel myself slipping back?

Theoretically, the results do last. Once you are on the right track, you will continue to move along in the right direction. In effect, you become your own therapist. And once the ball gets rolling, it is rolling downhill. It feels so good to be more assertive—or more open to feeling or more stable—for example, that you keep up the change and don't need the therapist. On the other hand, you should never feel that the door is permanently closed when you go off therapy. People often return at some point or points to work on different issues, or during times of crisis which sometimes frighten them into thinking they will go back to the way they were.

PART TWO

Common Problems—
Should You Have Psychotherapy?

CHAPTER SIX

Day-to-Day Relationships

SHYNESS AND LONELINESS

I can't tell you how lonely I am. During the week, when I'm working, it's not so bad. But most weekends I sit home alone and never speak to anyone besides the grocer and the mailman. Why don't I ever meet anybody?

There are a number of possibilities as to why you're so alone. In the first place, you may not be letting people know that you want to meet them. Are you passively waiting for people to introduce themselves to you? Do you then feel hurt or bitter when they are not as friendly as you would like them to be? If so, other people may be tuning into your negative feelings. And this, of course, greatly reduces the changes that anyone is going to start up a conversation, or think of inviting you along when making plans to go out to a movie or to dinner. As a result, you get caught in a vicious cycle of isolation. People who fall victim to this tend to rely on clichés such as "All the people I work with are very clique-ish" and "People aren't friendly toward me because they're jealous." If you repeatedly think this way, your attitude naturally tends to keep things just the way they are.

A second possibility is that you have come to feel so uncomfortable around people that you have fallen into an unconscious pattern of avoiding situations where you might meet someone. When was the last time you went somewhere by yourself? People find excuses for these avoidances such as "Parties are always too noisy," and they develop their own set routines. For example, I once treated an artist who worked alone all day and who spent his evenings and week-ends engaged in his only outside interest—reading.

Third, you may actually be having some preliminary social contact with people, but once you meet them, you do some-thing that puts them off. For example, you may be so self-conscious, or so concerned about whether they are going to like you or not, that you may not create a friendly, easygoing environment within which you and other people can enjoy each other.

Any one or any combination of these three possibilities can produce a situation in which you end up being very much by yourself.

I'm twenty-three years old, single, and I live alone. I enjoy spending a lot of time by myself reading and going to movies. Should I listen when my parents and other people nag me to be more social?

Not necessarily. First, ask yourself: Are you truly happier being alone most of the time, or would you really rather meet people? Some so-called "lonely" or "shy" people have been falsely labeled that way by their family members or friends. If this is what's happening in your case, it is this outside pres-sure to be more social that you are experiencing, rather than your own inward desire to have more contact and to establish relationships, with all that they entail.

Something else for you to consider is the possibility that your ability to be relatively self-sufficient socially somehow threatens those around you. Many people can't handle spending any time alone; in order to make themselves feel better about this, they tell you that *your* way is the wrong way. If you truly have little appetite for social contact, then you can try to learn to live with your solitude and get others to respect your wishes. Many people do choose to live lives of relative isolation and are quite happy.

I go out a lot and have plenty of friends, but whenever I walk into a room full of people, I get the feeling that everyone is looking at me, waiting for me to do something wrong. Would you call me a shy person?

Yes. You can be shy and still go out to various places. You can be shy and still talk to people. Some shy people are able to function socially, but that doesn't change the fact that at the core of everyone's shyness is the feeling of self-consciousness and the uneasy feeling that grows out of it.

Of course, everyone is *somewhat* aware of themselves and what others are thinking of them. But if you're a shy person, *all* you can think of when you walk into a room is how you appear to others, rather than relaxing and responding naturally to the other people around you. As a shy person, you often imagine that you will not handle things "correctly" and that others' thoughts are critical; this makes you feel uneasy. What happens next is that other people sense your uneasiness, and that interferes with *their* spontaneity. This creates an uncomfortable atmosphere for everyone and stifles the natural unfolding of relationships. Although some shy people avoid social situations, other people force themselves to go out but remain uncomfortable.

Isn't it true, though, that people don't go out of their way to talk to me because they just don't like me?

No, it's not that people don't like you. Rather, your shyness and uneasiness create a sense of tension and discomfort in other people. No one likes this feeling, so people may prefer not to spend their time with you because they feel your discomfort. You probably have many attractive qualities that are simply not coming across because your self-consciousness gets in the way.

I'm a forty-seven-year-old man, and for as long as I can remember, I have always felt self-conscious when I met someone who was very successful. Otherwise, I'm fine. Isn't everybody shy sometimes?

Almost everyone has experienced shyness at some time in their lives, even if it's only a mild instance. There are basically two kinds of shyness:

• *Situational Shyness* Situationally shy people experience their shyness only in very special situations. For example, meeting the president of the company would make most people feel some self-consciousness and concern about how they look to him or what they might say to him. Depending upon how often the situation occurs, this type of shyness may or may not be a big problem in their day-to-day lives.

• *General Shyness* For some people, however, shyness pervades their lives; they are called "generally shy." These people are enormously shy to the point where it limits almost every aspect of their lives involving contact with others, both socially and professionally. I have treated people who continually speak in a nervous, self-conscious way to almost everyone. Some have even been reluctant to order food in a local restaurant or to walk into a crowded room because they have felt all eyes turned their way to see who has entered.

I'm very relaxed with my friends and with men I'm not attracted to. But as soon as I come face to face with a good-looking guy, I become flustered. Why does this happen to me?

Being shy around people you find sexually attractive is a very common example of situational shyness. The reason for your feeling is that somewhere along the line you have picked up the idea that you are unacceptable and/or inadequate as a partner. You probably feel that you do not measure up to some female stereotype, and that a good-looking man who lives up to the male stereotype couldn't possibly be interested in you. You assume that he notices your feelings of inadequacy and so you feel self-conscious around him. Since you have not learned to feel inadequate in general, you don't feel shy around other people, such as your employers or friends.

I've been painfully shy all my life and now that I'm a widow, I'm afraid if I don't get over it, I'll be alone forever. Is it possible for me to overcome my shyness?

Probably—at least to some extent. Even though you, like other shy people, report that your shyness is a lifelong way of feeling, there is no reason for you to be discouraged and to think that you can't change the way you are. There are steps you can begin to take on your own (see below), and psychotherapy has also shown some quite impressive results in helping people overcome this problem. How successful you are will probably be affected by the severity and intensity of your shyness, but significant improvement certainly is possible. It is important to think positively. If you believe that you can't change, you may be predetermining your own behavior by making certain that you don't.

I've never liked my looks and have felt that they held me back from trying to meet people. Wouldn't I be less shy if I dressed better, lost weight, or had plastic surgery?

Although you may believe very strongly that one of these approaches will work, such approaches are rarely successful. Shyness is usually based on a deeply felt childhood pattern of thoughts, feelings, and behavior. Sometimes it can be partially helped by the steps you mention, but frequently these measures will only provide temporary relief from your shyness, as behavior patterns are often difficult to change.

I can't afford the time or money to go into therapy right now. What can I do on my own to get over my shyness?

If your problem is not severe—that is, if it occurs only in moderate amounts in certain situations—it is possible to work on your own:

    1. The first step is for you to recognize the fact that you are shy and to make the decision that you are going to attempt to change this.

2. Next, try to catch yourself being self-conscious as you think about going into situations where you are usually shy.

3. Then recognize that your self-consciousness comes from expecting criticism from yourself and others and that this criticism is not based on reality.

4. Try to imagine yourself going into these situations with a sense of self-trust and confidence. Practice feeling and acting confident—even if you do it alone at first—maybe in front of a mirror.

5. Make an attempt to place yourself in those situations that you have previously avoided. In other words, when you have made all those excuses about why you can't attend a party, this time go to the party.

6. Don't make inordinate demands of yourself—don't expect to be the life of the party. Be content at first to stand on the sidelines and just say hello to someone you know. Next time, say hello *and* make a few remarks. By repeatedly going to parties you will get used to that type of situation, will begin to feel more comfortable, and eventually will be able to be more outgoing. Remember: Take small steps, set easy goals, and be persistent.

If you can follow these simple steps, you should be able to make some headway on your problem. However, for severe cases of shyness, I strongly recommend psychotherapy. Because shyness is so common in our society and doesn't cause other people too much trouble, many people accept this problem in themselves and in others. That's why we often hear the phrase, "There's nothing wrong with him, he's just shy." The problem is often overlooked and so therapy is not recommended. But the problem can be very painful and very difficult to change on your own.

NONASSERTIVENESS

Everybody always walks all over me—my husband, my children, even the salesclerk at the supermarket. I can't stand being such a wimp. Why can't I stand up for myself?

This is a very common complaint, especially from women. As with other nonassertive people, you have learned to "sell out"—expressing your wishes and needs by trying to be easygoing and well liked and by avoiding fights and arguments. If you think in this kind of pattern, you probably also tell yourself how nice a person you are compared to other people who appear to be selfish and who are able to express their wishes and take more things for themselves. Nonassertive people always need to be liked by everyone, never to take for themselves without feeling selfish, always to avoid fights or confrontations, and so to allow other people to walk all over them.

Do you mean I'm nonassertive just because I'm nice, want to be liked, and try to avoid fighting?

Of course not. It is not a problem if you are nice and want to please other people *at times*. But you should ask yourself: How much of yourself are you sacrificing in order to be nice, to be liked, and to please others? Do you treat yourself at least as well as you treat others? Amazingly enough, the answer to the last question is frequently "no." In the process of trying not to disappoint others, you may be willing to disappoint yourself. If you are a nonassertive person, you usually give in to the preferences of others concerning a movie, a restaurant, and so on, and therefore are always willing to suffer the disappointment of not getting what you want in order that others rarely have to suffer. That's not even giving yourself a fair shake.

Another yardstick used to measure nonassertiveness is the degree to which you feel you want to express yourself but are unable to. Do you find that you have trouble expressing yourself? Oftentimes, the inability to express oneself is at the root of non-assertiveness.

You may also check out whether you find yourself giving in to requests that even you consider unreasonable. Or are you unable to effectively protect yourself against the nagging and repetitive criticism of others? Nonassertive people allow themselves to be taken advantage of by others because they are afraid to say no. They feel guilty on the rare occasions when they do speak up for themselves. As a result of their fear and guilt, they avoid coming into conflict with others.

Some of my friends and family tell me that I don't speak up for myself, but it doesn't seem to bother me. Do I have a problem?

If you really feel comfortable in the way you relate to people, then all you have to do is to learn to tell the people who keep telling you to change not to bother you any more. On the other hand, I find it hard to believe that a person who rarely expresses personal wishes, who always tiptoes around other people, doesn't mind it somewhat. We are all born with the wonderful ability to express our feelings and demand what we want from the world. If you inhibit this to a great degree, you usually suffer.

It's possible that you just don't recognize how much you are inhibited; in this case, the problem may come out in the form of some sort of physiological disorder. Headaches are especially common in nonassertive people (see "Psychosomatic Disorders," Chapter Fifteen). In any case, even if you are really suppressing your true feelings, ultimately you are the only one responsible for deciding whether you do or don't want to change.

Sometimes I have a terrible temper and go into a real rage. I say things I don't mean, and sometimes I become violent and even throw dishes at the wall. Can I still be considered nonassertive?

Absolutely. It is common for nonassertive people who inhibit their anger—either consciously or unconsciously—to at times feel completely outraged and furious. It is my belief that people who bend too often to other people's wishes develop a philosophy of feeling holier-than-thou, a degree of self-righteousness. When this self-image is thrown into question, they become outraged. For example, a young woman was in the habit of doing many favors, some unsolicited, for her friends. When on a rare occasion she asked a favor of a friend who could not or was unwilling to do it and so turned her down, the woman felt perfectly justified in becoming incredibly outraged that her friend had chosen not to reciprocate. Because she felt she had made so many sacrifices, even uncalled-for sacrifices, she thought, "After all I did for her, how dare she say no?" So, you see, extreme anger can be common in nonassertive people.

But can't assertiveness go too far? Some people are just too pushy.

Yes, it sometimes can, but perhaps like many people, you are confusing aggressiveness with assertiveness. However, they are somewhat separate entities.

Aggressiveness occurs when you attempt to gain self-esteem and to express your rights by ignoring another person's rights. It has to do with putting other people down, attacking them, humiliating and dominating them so that you feel good because another person feels bad.

Assertiveness has to do with speaking up for yourself, having self-esteem because of who you are—not because of who someone else is not. When you are being assertive, you are expressing your wishes in a direct, clear, and sometimes forceful way so that other people are aware of them and can take you into consideration.

If you have a history of being nonassertive with people and then begin to change, they sometimes object: "What has gotten into you?" They have gotten used to not having to take you into consideration, and it may take a period of adjustment for them to see you in this new way. Of course, assertiveness can be abused. If you are always speaking up for yourself forcefully and always pushing your ideas up front, you may be overdoing it. This type of behavior is self-indulgent, and can be very unpleasant to other people.

SHOULD YOU HAVE PSYCHOTHERAPY?

I realize that I'm not assertive enough, especially in social situations. I'm tired of having people ignore me. How can I become more assertive?

There are several steps that you can take to improve your ability to assert yourself.

1. *Pinpoint the Problem.* The first thing for you to do is to map out the problem. Don't demand change of yourself, and don't scold yourself. Look at the places in your life where you are nonassertive—where you are holding back your thoughts and feelings and not expressing yourself clearly and directly.

2. *What Are You Afraid Of?* It may also help to fathom exactly what in your mind is holding you back. I find what usually holds people back from being assertive is fear of another person getting angry or leaving. People tend to fantasize consequences out of proportion with reality and to exaggerate how much their speaking up will affect others. Sometimes it's almost a philosophy—a belief that you have no right to get good service from the delivery boy, or to be treated well by your husband, and that you will be selfish, arrogant, or aggressive if you speak up. If you can let yourself connect with the fact that you are having these thoughts, you can then try to talk yourself out of having them. Realize that if you do speak up, the other person may become annoyed, but most likely won't become as hurt or angry as you imagine.

3. *Look for the Easiest Place.* Then try to target the easiest place for you to change—*not* the most significant. For instance, if you are assertive with neither your husband nor the delivery boy, start with the delivery boy. Most people don't do this—their natural inclination is to start with what matters most to them, that makes it harder. But the chances are the fears that are holding you back are less prominent with the delivery boy than with your husband.

4. *Start Small.* For example, everyone in your group may

want to eat at an Italian restaurant, but you're in the mood for Chinese. In the past, you have never spoken up, and so you have always ended up eating spaghetti. You might start by simply saying that you'd prefer Chinese food. Even if you are overruled, at least you have spoken up. After you have become comfortable doing that, turn up the volume and try to say it a little more emphatically or louder, or to hold out longer. Many people find it helps them to rehearse being assertive beforehand either in their head, or out loud.

Although you should expect to stumble and fail occasionally, don't punish yourself—instead, make the task even smaller. And don't forget to reward yourself along the way, even if it's just a mental pat on the back.

I don't think I can overcome my nonassertiveness on my own. What are the advantages of going into psychotherapy for this problem?

During assertiveness training, which is often done in groups, assertiveness problems are identified in a systematic way. The therapy may help you to see the problem in places you are not at all aware of. Your therapist will help you figure out what is keeping you from being assertive—what the real root of your nonassertiveness is—in a very special way. He or she may employ certain psychological techniques such as implosion, role playing, or desensitization (see Chapter Two) to help you practice overcoming some of your inhibitions. You can also get the encouragement and support you need to practice assertiveness on the more difficult days. Analytic therapy will approach this problem in a broader way, looking at how your nonassertiveness fits more generally into your personality.

I encourage people to try assertiveness training because it has a high rate of success. Nonassertive people generally are highly motivated to change. Assertiveness, once learned, feels so good that you'll want to make it permanent.

Inhibition

I'm perfectly capable of saying what I mean during ordinary conversation. But I get tongue-tied during an emotional conversation or an argument, and only think of what to say afterward. I'm very frustrated and angry about this. Can it be helped?

Yes it can, and one way is by your understanding how this occurs. What usually happens—especially during heated confrontations—is that you become so self-conscious or worried about what's *going to* happen that you lose your natural ability to react to what *is* happening, and what the other person is saying at that moment. Your preoccupation with what the other person is going to say to you detracts from your thinking of how to respond. When the argument is over and you are no longer concerned with what the other person is thinking or saying, you then are able to think straight and come up with all the things you "should have" said. In essence, worry and fear have clouded your thinking.

With practice, you will be able to tell when such a situation is occurring and to make an effort to assert your own viewpoint. Sometimes a technique like desensitization (see Chapter Two) that focuses on retraining you to relax in certain situations can be very helpful.

I really love music, and I enjoy dancing when I'm alone at home listening to the radio. But when I go to a party or dance club, I just can't seem to loosen up. How can I overcome this inhibition?

Most people who feel inhibited dancing feel that others will be judging them critically. You are probably afraid that you will look foolish on the dance floor. Your fear then becomes a self-fulfilling prophecy: Because you expect to look clumsy and foolish, you tense up and as a result, you actually do move less gracefully. The next time you're out dancing, try to focus on the pleasure of dancing. Challenge the irrational thought that others are judging you harshly by telling yourself that most people are not even watching. Or that, if they are, they are probably not judging you harshly. Tell yourself that even if you are not a terrific dancer, it doesn't really matter. Take a good look at the other dancers. There are plenty of people who have loads of fun dancing even though they're not Baryshnikov.

In addition, you might consider taking dance lessons. Even though you may very well know how to dance, taking lessons can serve several purposes. It can give you the self-confidence you need, by forcing you into situations where you are dancing in the company of others. Gradually you will become more comfortable dancing around other people and overcome your inhibition. Your teacher and the other students may give you the positive reinforcement that you need to get over your fear of looking foolish. Finally, it may help you improve your own body movements. Any kind of dance class will serve this purpose. The point is to get in touch with your body as well as the music, to become more comfortable with moving your body, to relax and have fun.

CHAPTER SEVEN

Intimate Love Relationships

LACK OF INTIMACY AND LONG-LASTING RELATIONSHIPS

I'm a twenty-eight-year-old woman and I have lots of friends, but none of my romantic relationships ever lasts long. I'm not bad looking and I have a good personality—so why don't men stick around?

Your love relationships may be too short for a wide range of reasons.

• *Habit* To begin with, you may consistently choose people who are not interested in having long-term relationships.

• *Too-High Ideals* In addition, your expectations may be quite unrealistic. You may expect that you and your lover will always get along well, that all your needs will be satisfied by just one person, and that you will always feel wonderful about each other. Unfortunately, the kind of relationship you are envisioning exists only in dreams and fairy tales. Consequently, your own are bound to fall short of your expectations. Each time a relationship meets with some difficulties, you might back off from the other person involved, as a result of your disappointment and frustration.

• *Fear of Commitment* It is also possible that you are afraid of the commitment involved in long-term relationships. Do you eventually feel trapped after you've experienced closeness with someone? Instead of seeing the possibility for you and your partner to grow within your relationship, you may think that you have to be alone to experience growth.

But most of my friends also have trouble establishing solid, long-term relationships. It's not just me. It seems that times are different now—it's just harder for everyone to stay with a person. Isn't this true?

Yes; there are a lot of sociological reasons which have contributed to the overall brevity of today's relationships. These include:

- The mobility of the society
- Sexual promiscuity
- Busy schedules
- The accessibility of divorce
- Higher income for women

All of these contribute to the statistical facts of shorter relationships. It is my belief, however, that many psychological factors also intervene, especially for those who find themselves chronically involved in short-term relationships. While we may not be able to do much individually about other factors, we can work on ourselves to improve our chances of having a steady, meaningful relationship.

I'm over forty years old and I want to get married, but I can't find the right person. I'm never satisfied with the people I date— why do they always seem too short, or fat, or overbearing, or dull, or old, or poor?

There are basically two possibilities that come to mind.

1. *High Hopes* You may have a set of extraordinarily high expectations, which may have been transmitted from your family or through the media. As a result, you may have in your mind a picture of the perfect mate—and in order for you to be happy with someone they have to fit that stereotype. The fallacy here is that although you might prefer that your date or spouse be a little taller or richer, this really wouldn't have to interfere with your love, appreciation, and happiness to a serious degree. We all have certain standards and expectations about people we go out with or marry. However, if you stick to your expectations too rigidly, you find that almost everyone falls short of the mark in some way. Unless you are willing to recognize that some of the "stan-

dards" won't really affect your life together, you will continue to reject people and then wonder why your life seems so empty.

2. *Secret Fears* The second possibility is that you are overly critical as a means of keeping people at bay, to cover up your secret wish to be alone or your fear of being too close. As much as you say you want to have a relationship, you may be using your high standards as an excuse to avoid it. You may feel threatened at the possibility of having a close relationship. You may worry that you may become vulnerable or feel guilty that you may not live up to the other person's expectations or may hurt a mate in some way. Sometimes a part of a person really wants to be with someone, but another part is afraid of it happening, and the fearful part wins out.

I have treated many patients who felt that they were getting older, but just couldn't seem to meet anybody. What I've frequently done in the therapy is to focus on these feelings of vulnerability and guilt. Explore in your mind: How terrible would it be if you do love someone and are rejected? How terrible would it be if you do get close to someone and in some way disappoint or hurt that person? Aren't both of these possibilities acceptable and worthwhile in terms of taking the risk of really caring for someone?

My husband and I love each other very much but we never seem to talk about anything that's important—only superficial day-to-day business like the kids' grades and what happened at work. I feel that something is missing. Am I right—is there anything wrong with this?

There's nothing wrong with this type of relationship if both of you are comfortable with the level of interaction that you have. Some people just don't require the verbal intimacy that others do.

On the other hand, sometimes one person would prefer a deeper level of verbal intimacy and is upset when the other doesn't respond to his or her promptings. Both men and women can have this fear of intimacy; however, men seem to be affected more than women and sometimes they don't even realize it. Some men cover up their fear of exposing themselves in a relationship by feeling primarily committed to their work, or driven to see other women. Others may cover up fear and self-doubts by expressing themselves with anger, by making a joke out of it, or by changing the subject.

If you have been able to communicate more intimately with other people in your life, perhaps you are having trouble now because your husband was brought up not to communicate, not to express himself—particularly in regard to his "softer" or "weaker" thoughts and feelings. Consequently, he censors many of his thoughts. This alienates him from the people he lives with and puts him more and more in the position of going through the motions. The best way to change this is not through criticism of your husband, but through gently pointing out his behavior and giving him a positive example. Talk more yourself about other things or try to get him to open up more.

My friends tease me and don't give me any sympathy when I tell them about my problems with the women I date. They say of course I always have the same problems because I always go out with the same type of woman. Why do I keep going out with the same type of person, even when I know that's not the type for me? How can I stop?

Going out with the same type of person means you can stay the same. It allows you to act in the same old comfortable groove. Since you are unhappy with this habit, what you might do is to consciously start looking for someone who is different. However, you must also try to realize that being with someone different will force *you* to be different. You must be prepared to make a commitment to yourself to undergo that change and expansion of your personality. This is usually not as easy as it seems.

An example of this is a woman patient of mine who always goes out with very strong, successful, and somewhat domineering men. She eventually comes to resent these aspects of their personalities, and finds herself wishing that she would meet a man who is "nicer, sweeter, and more understanding." When she does go out with someone more considerate, less powerful, less domineering, she is initially enthusiastic. But in this type of relationship, she is more of an equal; she has to make decisions, she has to be more mature, and she has to take some of the responsibility for what happens in the relationship. It is difficult for her to play this equal role, more difficult than to be with the domineering man with whom she can play the more passive, dependent, and childlike role.

The answer here is to break out of the mold gradually. Begin by finding someone who is *slightly* different from your usual type, and to expect that even though you want this type of relationship in the long run, in the short run it's going to make you uncomfortable.

BOREDOM, INFIDELITY, JEALOUSY

I've been married for nine years, and although my husband and I love each other, I've recently realized that our relationship has gotten boring. Although I don't like it, I guess this is to be expected. Is this the usual case in marriages?

To some degree it is understandable. It's hard to keep the same level of excitement going with someone whom you are used to and sure of. On the other hand, it doesn't have to be this way if you don't want it to be—there are several ways to keep a relationship interesting and creative.

Try being more intimate, more self-disclosing, and more adventuresome with each other. What can you do that would present another side of you—one your husband has never seen before? Try new things on your own so you remain an interesting, lively person; explore new things together so you remain an interesting, lively couple. This will surely create a sense of continued growth and increasing closeness between the two of you.

It is very easy to get stuck in the same old comfortable rut and then blame it on the other person. You may also find it tempting to try to solve the problem by going outside the relationship, instead of seeing any possibility for enhancing what's already there. This, I would like to point out to you, is rarely the answer.

I recently found out that my husband is having an affair with a woman he works with. We've got a beautiful home, two lovely children—I've always thought we were happy together. I'm completely dumbfounded by the news. Should I confront him with it?

I am reluctant to give this type of specific advice without knowing more details. However, I sense from your question that it is very difficult for you to accept this new development in your relationship. Therefore, if you don't confront him, it will probably have a major effect on you and most likely be quite harmful to your relationship in the long run. So, in essence, it seems you have very little choice.

I understand that this may be a very difficult, unpleasant task for you and may lead to a great deal of hostility between you and your husband. But choosing to confront the transgressor is ultimately much less costly than choosing not to. Of course, situations like this do sometimes rupture relationships. But at other times they provide an opportunity to air your feelings, or talk about a problem that has been long in the making, thus clearing the air for a new, positive beginning.

My wife is very jealous. She won't let me out of the house except to go to the office and wants to know every little detail about what I did and where I went. I'm afraid her distrust is going to ruin our marriage. How can I make her feel more secure?

My first question to you is: Are you doing anything to make her feel insecure? Have you done something—made innuendos or flirted with other women—to arouse her suspicions or fan the flames of her jealous tendencies?

If you haven't, you can begin by assuring her of your feelings for her. If your wife's jealousy is as obsessive as it sounds, however, this will have only a marginal effect. You and she should sit down together and try to understand what in her mind is making her so jealous and insecure, apart from anything you are actually doing. Often in these cases, the jealous person does not feel worthy of the other person's fidelity, and so is always waiting for the ax to fall because the jealous one feels it *should* fall. You will probably find it helpful to go for couples or individual therapy. You are right to worry about your marriage: In the long run, a situation such as the one you describe can pose a very serious threat to the relationship.

My brother is very jealous of his wife, who is really devoted to him and wouldn't dream of cheating. Why is he so possessive and jealous?

Possessiveness is only part of the picture in most cases of jealousy. Possessiveness usually shows an attempt to reduce the possibility that the person will have the opportunity to be unfaithful. Your brother may also be using possessiveness to make unlikely *the appearance to others* that he is being cheated on. However, jealousy has many beginnings. As was mentioned in the answer to the preceding question, your brother's own sense of unworthiness may be at the root of his possessiveness. Or he may be projecting his own desires or actions onto the other person, thinking that if he wants to cheat, his wife must also.

Another possibility is that he is "catastrophizing" about the possibility of being left by his wife. There is always *some* chance that she is going to abandon him. But your jealous brother may so inordinately dread abandonment that he cannot stop thinking about it. Ironically, he has gotten himself caught up in a vicious cycle: The more jealous he is, the more he oppresses his wife; his behavior gives her a reason to leave him.

Most people under certain circumstances feel some jealousy. But the question is always a matter of degree and whether it is obsessive. The ultimate question is: Is there real cause for the jealousy? Or is the person constantly thinking about the possibility of being abandoned and so precluding good times and good feelings from occurring in the relationship?

Now that we have a baby, my husband says I love the baby more than I love him. He almost sounds jealous—should I pay more attention to him?

First of all, it is conceivable that you are not paying enough attention to him and that your husband really *is* jealous of the baby. You may be so absorbed with matters relating to the baby that you are neglecting your relationship with your husband. Perhaps you have been told all your life that motherhood is the most important thing there is and as a result have basically abandoned your role of wife in favor of your role as mother. You should examine this possibility, and if this is what is happening, realize that it is really unfair to your husband and that the best thing for you to do is to discuss it with him.

On the other hand, your husband my be spoiled. Before the baby arrived, he may have gotten a lot of attention from you. It is not surprising then, depending on his personality, that he feels put out by the new member of the family. The solution here may be to confront him with this possibility. Perhaps you can help your husband come to the understanding that a decrease in your attention toward him doesn't mean a decrease in your feelings for him. In addition, you might try to get him more involved with the baby so that he gets his share of attention from the baby too. As he invests more in his fatherhood, your parental roles will become more equal and he won't be waiting in the background to get attention from you—he'll be busy himself!

BICKERING AND FIGHTING

My husband and I seem to fight all the time—usually over nothing, like the laundry or where to go for dinner. I hate it, but our friends tell us we love to fight. Could this be true?

Most repetitive fights that couples have are not about what they seem to be. Underlying issues include, for example:

Suppressed Anger: Anger about big, important issues remains unexpressed, but eventually comes out as fights about unimportant issues.

Power: How power is going to be shared, who is going to make the decisions that affect the couple.

Scapegoating: One member takes out anger about something outside the relationship on the partner.

So it is not surprising that couples throw themselves wholeheartedly into fights about seemingly trivial issues.

You and your husband may fight a great deal because you haven't learned how to resolve differences in any other way. You both may feel that you have to win to get your way, instead of understanding the nature of compromise. You may never have learned how to express your wishes without aggressively attacking the other person. You may also have learned from your family that fighting is one of the ways that people use to make contact with each other. So although you may not love fighting as your friends say you do, you may find it invaluable.

I'm so frightened when my wife and I fight—doesn't fighting mean we're going to break up?

Although it may cause general unhappiness between you and your wife, fighting does not necessarily mean that your relationship is going to break up. Some couples have been together for years, during which they have fought bitterly. This, of course, is an extreme, but some fighting is unavoidable in all relationships. In fact, when a couple never fights, I tend to wonder what they are covering up and keeping from each other.

However, if your fighting worries you, ask yourself if the fighting is frequent or repetitive. Does it end in bitterness toward each other which then affects other areas of your relationship? If so, this type of conflict is in no way a learning process during which there is a positive change, and counseling or therapy can go a long way in improving the situation. When fighting has become excessive and unproductive, it's usually advisable to determine the underlying causes and to look for other ways to relate to each other.

My family never fought among themselves—in fact, they rarely spoke to each other at all. Now I get very hurt when my husband yells at me because I think it means he doesn't love me any more.

In my experience, yelling or arguing is not a likely way for him to show you this. Some people—and your husband is probably one of them—have been brought up in a family where yelling and fighting is an acceptable way to show displeasure or anger, at least at times. If you were not brought up this way, you may be misinterpreting his intent. You should try to discuss this with your husband, particularly as it relates to your fears concerning his yelling. This will not necessarily get him to stop completely, but at least it may cause him to yell less often. In addition, you may come to understand what he is feeling and what it means when he yells at you. Most likely his shouting means that he is *temporarily* angry with you, but that this has nothing to do with how much he loves you. Having talked it over, you can then consider whether *some* yelling is more tolerable for you. If not, you can take the next step, which is to leave the room when he yells at you.

I think we have a good marriage, but my husband and I do have some problems from time to time. What makes for a healthy relationship anyway? How do we know when our problems are getting serious?

All relationships have troubles from time to time and many of the same problems are repeated in different forms throughout the relationship. In any committed long-lasting relationship there is a general sense of mutual respect and trust, a willingness to confront problems and to compromise, which places the problems in perspective and allows them to be either resolved or contained.

You know your problems are getting serious, however, when they start to spill over into the positive aspects of your relationship and to outweigh or spoil whatever you have together that's good. This is a sure sign that they are getting too serious to be ignored and that you should consider taking steps to resolve things, even going so far as to enter couples therapy or see a marriage counselor. For example, you and your husband might argue from time to time over the money spent for purchases. If at some point the bitterness cannot be resolved even partially, it may loom so large that you stop having sex; next, you may avoid spending time together; and so on until the arguments and bad feelings permeate every aspect of your relationship.

Another cause for concern is when you have problems that simply cannot be discussed, either because they are too volatile, or possibly taboo for some other reason. In this kind of situation, the problems usually fester and don't result in arguments. Instead, you withdraw psychologically or physically, which also destroys relationships.

Isn't love enough to solve all our problems?

Not really. Love is having a deep, positive, caring feeling for another person. While this certainly can help minimize some disagreements and provide the motivation for dealing with others, problems may still exist, and you still need some kind of negotiation and communication skills before you can arrive at a mutually acceptable solution. For example, you may love your husband but object to his working hours. Or, you and your husband may love each other, but may have very different ideas about how to raise your children. Love is clearly not enough to surmount these kinds of problems—you really need to sit down and work at solutions.

CHAPTER EIGHT

Family Problems

CHILDREN AND TEENS

I have three teenagers, aged fifteen, sixteen, and eighteen. They've always been good kids, but now they're driving me crazy—they talk back to me, they stay out until after midnight, and I never know where they are. My parents never had this trouble with me. Am I doing something wrong as a parent?

In order to understand your teen-aged children, you must understand what adolescence is all about. Adolescence often involves a tremendous upheaval, both physically and psychologically. Teen-agers are in the throes of asserting their own autonomy. They are at the point in their lives when they are beginning to form and express their own opinions and values about the world, and this usually means going through some period of rebellion against their parents. This is not true of all teen-agers, and it may not have been true of you. If you rebelled at all, you may have done so in a more quiet way. But you must keep in mind that things are not the way they used to be—your current family situation may be somewhat different from the family situation in which you grew up.

If your teens' rebellion remains moderate and is not really destructive or causing you inordinate amounts of embarrassment or grief, your best course of action is to accept the situation. Yes, there may be a generation gap between you and your teen-agers. Yes, they may be groping for their own identities and independence by not listening to all your instructions and directions. But this conflict over authority is normal and in some ways desirable, as it can be a sign of separation and growth. It does not necessarily reflect poorly on your abilities as a parent.

SHOULD YOU HAVE PSYCHOTHERAPY?

I've always been very understanding of my daughter and tried to make her happy. But now she's rewarding me by getting bad grades and hanging out with degenerates. She's just too wild—how can I handle her?

If you are not exaggerating and your daughter really is extremely rebellious, extremely negative at school or home, and extremely angry at you and your husband, more may be going on here than the simple struggle to establish autonomy. Sometimes children can suffer from too much freedom and too much responsibility for their own actions at an early age. Your daughter may be trying to provoke you to act like parents: to set limits and establish rules for acceptable behavior, and to more firmly and consistently govern her life.

Another possibility is that your rebellious teen-ager is really reacting to a conflict that is going on between her parents. You might examine this in terms of the possibility that either you or your husband is somehow encouraging the child to act in a disruptive or aggravating way to the other parent.

An example of this is the family I once treated who had a very rebellious teen-age son. The family had a very verbal and domineering mother and a relatively passive and submissive father. Family therapy revealed that although both parents *said* they wished the son were less rebellious, the father enjoyed his son's rebelliousness because it frustrated his wife so much. The therapy attempted to remove the child from the conflict between the parents and to encourage the father to confront his wife directly.

You should examine your own family relationships and interactions. Try to talk to your child and find out what she is feeling and why she feels a need to rebel to such a degree. If your own efforts at straightening out problems with your rebellious teen-ager don't seem to be enough, I recommend that you look into family therapy or individual therapy.

One of my children is very talkative and friendly, but the other is withdrawn and quiet. I worry about him; how can I get him to talk more?

It is not unusual for children in the same family to be quite different from each other. These differences may become noticeable at a surprisingly early age. In fact, many experts believe that genes may in part cause these differences in temperament and personality. We are unique individuals from the very beginning of our lives.

However, you are right to be concerned if your quiet child is more than just different from your outgoing child. Some children do become seriously withdrawn. It is possible that he is shy, and because of this is not fitting in with his sibling and friends. It is also conceivable that your child is depressed—depression can occur at any age. If the problem seems to fall into either the shyness or the depression category, I suggest that you consider family or individual therapy.

My oldest daughter is eight years old and although she loved her new baby brother at first, she has lately begun to tease and fight with him. How can I handle this sibling rivalry?

First, you must understand that all sibling rivalry comes down to children competing with one another to be best-loved by their parents. Depending upon the age difference, sibling rivalry may take the form of depression, or of hostility and regressive behavior, or of teasing or annoying behavior or other expressions of anger toward the younger child. It may be disguised as temper tantrums, sleep disturbances, crankiness, or other disturbed behavior as an unconscious attempt to get back a larger share of your attention.

Although it may be difficult for you to feel affectionate toward a naughty child, this is often the best first course of action. Simply assuring the older one that you still love her may be enough to cause at least the worst symptoms of rivalry to disappear. If you interfere with your children's battles and take the side of the smaller one, it will only tend to perpetuate the situation.

Remember, it is not possible for children to live together without some friction. Nor is it desirable. Brothers and sisters provide each other with invaluable opportunities to sample real life. Through their everyday conflicts with each other, your son and daughter are learning that, although it may not be easy, problems between people can be worked out.

My twelve-year-old is getting terrible grades, but he's smart and I know he's capable of doing much better. How can I get him to study more?

Two reasons come to mind as to why your child is not studying as much as you think he should.

• *Different Priorities and Values* It's highly likely that studying doesn't seem as important to him as other things in his life. His values might be closer to those of his friends than to your values.

If this is the case with your son, punishing him for not studying most likely will not increase the amount of studying he's going to do. It may be better to set up a schedule where he earns the right to do things that he really enjoys in exchange for putting in a certain number of study hours. Let your child know why you believe it's important that he study, and help him to understand how he might benefit from it. I think it's generally a good idea to make study as much of a pleasurable experience as possible. Compare studying to something he enjoys like playing basketball. Stress the fact that just as he gets satisfaction and joy from practicing to improve his game, he can get a feeling of accomplishment by studying.

• *Too Much Pressure* Another notion is that some children don't study because they feel tremendously pressured to do so. When there's too much pressure, most of us become negative about what we're doing, and children are no exception. If your son has received the message that getting good grades is very, very important, studying takes on a negative connotation. While he's studying, he may be worried about how much he's going to remember, or how well he's going to do. Of course this preoccupation interferes with his ability to retain what he studies and encourages procrastination.

So ask yourself if you are giving your child too much pressure. If so, depressurize the studying atmosphere. Let him know that you would like to see him learn his lessons, but that getting a high grade is not the most important thing. It is more productive for you to teach him to enjoy the process of learning and be self-motivated than to coerce and threaten him.

Both my children are having difficulties at school. I wish I knew what was going on. Should I talk to their teachers or a child guidance counselor?

Meeting with the teachers and the child guidance counselor can prove very helpful in giving you some insight into the specific difficulties your child may be having in the learning process. During this meeting, just remember that it's important to understand where your children are coming from rather than to try to employ force (or to try to get the school to employ force) in this situation. Additionally, it may be helpful if you describe your family's home environment to the counselor. He or she can get pertinent information from the teachers and tests, but also needs information about your children's life outside of school to complete the picture.

I'm very worried about my son. He'd rather stay alone in his room watching television than do anything else. He really doesn't have any friends. He's very good, and never complains, but we worry. Recently, I learned from his teachers that he has difficulties in school. Can you tell me why?

Children can sometimes experience severe psychological disorders. I'm not saying this in order to scare you, but to alert

you to the fact that some parents misunderstand this behavior and write it off, believing that all children will grow
out of things and that all they need is time. This is not always
true. If your child is isolated, depressed, and withdrawn he
will benefit from psychotherapy, and I think you should
consider it.

There can be any number of reasons why your child is
having difficulties in school. For example, he may be responding to something that is going on in the family. Or he
may suffer from being teased or ignored by his schoolmates. I
think the danger here is that although many parents tend to
worry too much about their children, others are not concerned and aware enough. Don't make the mistake of brush-
ing off his difficulties because your child is not a "problem"
in terms of getting poor school grades or causing difficulties
at home. The so-called "good" child is often the one whose
problems are overlooked.

*Other kids don't seem to like my child. She tries very hard, and
I've given some parties, but after a party is over, she still doesn't
have enough friends. Am I doing too much or too little?*

In a situation like this, sometimes it's the parents who have
the problem, not the child. You might have overly ambitious
expectations for your daughter and want her to be the most
popular kid on the block. If this is the case, and your child is
not meeting your expectations, you should back off and
allow her to find her own social niche.

One of the most frequent causes of childhood isolation is
too much dependence on the family. Your child needs a
certain amount of independence if she is going to operate
adequately with other children. The solution here lies not in
forging ahead and trying to create an environment in which
your child will be liked (as in the case of giving parties);
rather it lies in allowing your child to go out on her own and
have her own experiences with her peers, even if they are not
all positive.

PARENTS AND IN-LAWS

Even though I'm a thirty-year-old adult, and have been living on my own for ten years, my parents and I still fight about how I live my life. Why don't they realize I have a life of my own to live?

Your parents may feel a need to keep you as a child—it may give them a sense of purpose, it may give them a sense of superiority, or it may simply be the only way they know to express how much they care for you. I suggest that you sit down with your parents and discuss the matter. Tell them you realize that they probably mean well, but that their attempts to impose their standards on your life tend to alienate you. Let them know that you would appreciate it if they could relate to you in some other way.

In addition, you may unknowingly encourage your parents' behavior, and if so, this is something you can alleviate. By overreacting to their attempts to offer advice, you could be causing these arguments to be prolonged. So one thing you might learn to do is to overlook their remarks to some degree. Try to accept them politely with a passing acknowledgment, but then go ahead and do what you want to do.

How can I stop my mother-in-law from always butting in and telling me how to raise the children? My husband always takes her side.

This is a problem of asserting yourself (see Chapter Six) with both your mother-in-law and your husband. You should try to tell your husband's mother that, although you love and respect her, you are uncomfortable about her giving you advice about the children, and you would prefer to learn by your own mistakes. I also recommend your being assertive with your husband and letting him know how his behavior in this matter is making you feel. Tell him that he doesn't necessarily have to side with you, but that you would appreciate it if he would allow you to work out the relationship with your mother-in-law without his interference.

SHOULD YOU HAVE PSYCHOTHERAPY?

I love my in-laws, but I don't know what to do when my husband fights with his parents. I feel as though I'm caught in the middle.

Basically, you need to allow them to work out their difficulties. Under no circumstances should you fall into the trap of taking sides. Instead, be sympathetic to all parties, recognizing the pain each is experiencing and never once concluding that any party is the villain. Each side may try to draw you in, in hopes of gaining your support, but you don't have to feel obligated to align yourself.

I'm thirty-five years old, but I don't feel ready to get married or have children. I like my freedom. My parents tell me to grow up, but why can't I just go on concentrating on my career and enjoying my life the way it is?

You can. There's nothing inherently wrong in never getting married, or in getting married late in life, or in never having children. It seems to me that your problem is not your decision to remain single or to postpone having children; instead, it is the great amount of pressure you are experiencing as the result of your parents' attitudes toward your decision.

The challenge here is for you to stand firm in the midst of all this pressure. You might want to have a long talk with them and explain to them, in a very clear and direct way, exactly what you feel. Add that this is too important a question in your life for you to succumb to their pressure. Let them know that their pressuring you does not affect you in a positive way, and ask them to try to understand your viewpoint and to stop trying to get you to change your life.

My parents are so conservative and closed-minded that I've had to hide from them a lot of the details about my life. Now I wonder— should I confide in them? Should I let them know what my life is really like so we can be closer?

While it's true that we all tell little white lies to avoid pain and confrontation, not telling the truth on a wide-scale basis can create tension and lower the quality of communication between us and the other people who mean so much to us. You have sensed this and it is understandable that you want to improve the situation.

However, before you reveal anything to your parents, I suggest that you take a good hard look at your motives. Do you really want to tell all in order to feel closer to your parents—or do you merely want to relieve yourself of the frustration incurred by leading, in a sense, "a secret life"? If you truly desire greater intimacy, begin by finding out how much they know already. It may be more than you have suspected! Then ask them if *they* would be interested in knowing more about you. They might say no, and you of course should respect their wishes.

CHAPTER NINE

Job Problems

BOSS AND CO-WORKERS

I've been with the company for six years and I'd hate to leave. But my new boss doesn't appreciate the work I do and treats me badly. How can I let him know I'm upset about this? Should I change jobs?

Why don't you try to work things out before you leave your job? Try to present the things that are bothering you to the boss in an assertive way. You might say, for instance, "I've been unhappy with my job lately because I feel that you are not appreciating all that I'm putting into it." Or, "I didn't get the promotion I've been expecting. Can you tell me why that didn't happen?"

Most people are afraid to say these things because they assume they are going to make the boss angry at them. But if you speak assertively, in a way that expresses a feeling or requests information without pointing an accusatory finger at him (for example, do not say "You so-and-so, how come you didn't give me a raise?"), he will most likely respond positively. At least he will hear what you are saying and may be willing to give you some kind of thoughtful response in a respectful manner.

A few months ago I fell in love with my boss, who is a powerful, impressive man. We began to have an affair and now all the other people at the office know it and are jealous and paranoid. Did I make a big mistake?

It's hard for me to tell you that falling in love was a mistake; romantic love is a wonderful, important aspect of our lives. However, office affairs do have their pluses and minuses. On the minus side, they cause gossip, low morale, low productivity, and complaints among colleagues. They may ultimately jeopardize your job and/or career. However, whether it's your boss, co-worker, or subordinate that you get involved with, the office is a logical place to find romance. Working side by side with people every day allows you to get to know them in a more natural, gradual, and stimulating way than in other settings such as on vacations or at singles bars. So becoming involved with the boss was understandable. Your affair may not have been a mistake, but not being more discreet about it was.

What do I do if my intimate relationship with my boss ends?

Unlike the usual relationship, when an office romance breaks up, you still have to see each other and work with each other every day. I advise you to try to keep the breakup as civil as possible, and to maintain a considerate, rather than a vindictive, office relationship even though the emotional climate has changed. Try to be businesslike at the office, and if you need to further discuss or rehash what happened, really do your best to separate that from the business part of the relationship.

I can't seem to get along with any of my bosses and I end up changing jobs often. I've had five jobs in the last three years, and employers are beginning to raise their eyebrows when they see my résumé. How can I change this before my career goes down the tubes?

The most obvious issue here is your difficulty in dealing with and accepting authority. This may show up in other situations in your life, as, for example, in dealing with government officials. One solution to the problem is to go into business for yourself and avoid dealing with authority. However, if the problem is severe, you will find that even when you don't work under someone else's supervision, you will still occasionally encounter authority.

You might question yourself about which issues surrounding the idea of authority are giving you problems. In many cases the problem can be traced back to childhood. One child's solution to repressive, stern, autocratic parents may be to submit to them. Another solution—and the one that you seem to have adopted—is to be rebellious and assert your autonomy in negative ways, for instance, by contradicting your parents or doing the exact opposite of what they say. You may have continued this pattern throughout your life with other authority figures.

Since your problem seems severe, I would recommend therapy as a means of disentangling this issue. If it was less severe, you might try to make a lot of contact with your boss; forcing yourself to be friendly or social might counteract some of your negative feelings. Developing empathy could help you come to understand the boss's point of view and take away the "me-against-him" aspect of your relationship.

One of my co-workers is very nice to me to my face, but I found out that he's been saying bad things about me and my work behind my back. I need this job and I have to get along with him; but how do I keep from exploding?

Since you have to get along with the person and you want to avoid a confrontation that will end in bitterness or estrangement, let's begin by putting yourself in his shoes. Obviously you are doing something that bothers him, either justifiably or unjustifiably. For some reason—either because of you or of something in his own personal history—this person has the habit of not being direct. The best thing to do is to take the initiative and address him directly. Tell him that you understand that he has been saying some negative things about you, and this must mean that you are doing something that bothers him. Make it clear that although you will not necessarily change what you are doing, you would like him to tell you face to face what it is, so that you can discuss it. That gives him permission to approach you in a direct way, which he has not been allowing himself to do.

When I work on projects with other people, some of them don't pull their own weight. I'm getting tired of covering up for them and doing their jobs for them; should I confront them with this?

Where does this need to cover up for people come from? Not only are you doing your own job, but theirs as well, and then covering up for them on top of it. Obviously, this bothers you. So let's begin by your making clear to yourself and your colleagues that you will do only your share of the work. You are clearly taking on too much responsibility, and you feel that if another person doesn't do the job, then you must do it. Maybe what's necessary is for you to allow the situation to go somewhat awry, so your supervisor will notice this and confront it. You should also make it clear with your co-workers that you won't cover up for anyone. If asked, you should present to your supervisors, as honestly and clearly as possible, exactly how much you have done and how much other people have done.

On the other hand, it is also possible that you are working only a little bit harder than other people, and that they are getting away with this. It is an interesting natural phenomenon that when people work in groups, they don't work equally—and they never will. Life is not fair, nor are things equal, and if you are measuring exactly what you are doing against what other people are doing, you are wasting a lot of energy. Try to accept the fact that life is not fair and that you may simply be a harder, more conscientious worker than some other people; that you should not spend a great deal of energy trying to balance things out perfectly.

WORK HABITS AND ATTITUDES

I have trouble getting up most mornings, and sometimes I even sleep through the alarm. I take forever to get ready and as a result I'm always late for work. Does this mean I hate my job and I should quit?

Not necessarily, but it may mean you resent it. If you hated your job outright, you would probably be more aggressively hostile, and end up leaving it or being fired. The late-for-work syndrome is really a reflection of your feelings that something is unfair about aspects of your work. (Mere unpleasantness is usually acceptable, if we think it is fair.) Try to confront the unfairness and see what you can do to correct it. If you can't correct it, try to accept the notion of unfairness—that you may not be able to do that much about it, but that perhaps things aren't actually so unfair anyway. (See also "Hostility" in Chapter Ten.) You may also find it interesting to note that on the rare occasions when the unfair work world is unfair in your favor, you don't object at all.

I see other people in my office getting promoted, but I seem to be stuck in my position. I've been in this job for five years and I'm a good worker. My friends tell me I'm not getting ahead because I just have no ambition. Is this true?

It sounds to me as if you *do* have ambition because you seem to be unhappy that it is not being satisfied by a promotion. What may be happening is that you are not communicating your desire to get ahead to your employers, and so they do not see you as a person who is particularly ambitious. I would suggest that you speak with your employers and let them know that you wish to be promoted. Ask them to tell you what they feel you need to do in order to be considered for promotion. If you find that your employers do not consider you suitable material for a higher position and there is nothing you can do to change their impression, then you can look for another job where you will have a better chance for promotion.

Every time I'm given an important assignment at work, I screw up somehow. I'm well-liked, so I haven't gotten fired, but how can I stop ruining my chances of having a successful career?

There may be a number of reasons why you are screwing up. One may be anxiety. My guess is that you become very anxious to do the project well, and this anxiety works against you, causing you to make errors. So I would try to reduce the anxiety in some way. (See Chapter Eleven for more information on reducing anxiety.)

Another possibility is that you unconsciously don't believe you deserve the success that you would earn if you did well and so you are sabotaging yourself. Try to look inside yourself to see if this is a possibility. If you can't improve the situation, and if it is important to you that you do change it, I suggest that you try psychotherapy to learn how to be more self-deserving.

WORKAHOLIC

I try very hard, but I can't get my mind off my work. I know it's wrong, and my wife resents it, but that doesn't seem to matter. Am I a workaholic?

If you not only can't get your mind off work, but put in excessive time at the office, I would say that you meet the definition of a workaholic. If your "workaholism" is mostly your constantly thinking about your work, it is actually an obsession (see Chapter Fourteen). There are basically two reasons why people become workaholics.

• *Fear of Failure* Workaholics often have a tremendous fear of failing. They believe they have to work twice as hard as everybody else just to keep even. You might explore in your own life whether this is true and where your feeling of inferiority comes from.

• *Avoidance of Unpleasant Situations* Workaholics also may be trying to avoid other situations. For example, you may be more comfortable at work than at home. Naturally, you choose to spend more time at work.

I treated a bank vice-president who would never go home. Although he said he wanted to go home, he also said he felt the bank would collapse without him. We discovered that he had a great deal of prestige and satisfaction at work because of his position. But at home his wife was a tyrant, and he was unable to deal with her. He consequently chose to avoid home and family. His therapy involved helping him to deal more effectively and comfortably with his wife. That coincidentally resulted in his reducing his working hours.

I think I'm a workaholic, but I don't want to go into therapy because it would take too much time. Is psychotherapy the only answer for workaholics?

No. To begin with, some workaholics do not define their focus as a problem, or they choose to do nothing about it; they continue to be workaholics and are very productive in their businesses. If you do want to change, an alternative to psychotherapy is to join one of the self-help groups that exist across the country. Many people find such Workaholics Anonymous groups to be helpful. Or, on your own, you can try to make a real effort to reduce your time at work in the simplest, even superficial way: by disciplining yourself to limit your hours there.

I really love my work—is everyone who works hard a workaholic?

No—some people are just healthy hard workers. The difference lies in the motivation. A hard worker freely chooses to put in long hours because he or she primarily is interested in personal and professional growth. For these people, work is stimulating and gratifying.

True *workaholics,* however, seem to have no choice. They are driven, compelled to act this way by forces they may not understand. There is about them an aura of grim determination rather than satisfaction. Workaholics often feel deprived of love and work not for the sheer pleasure of it, but in order to gain the approval and acceptance of others. Work seems to be their whole life; if they are not at work, they feel worthless. They are addicted to work in the same way alcoholics are addicted to alcohol. Ironically, workaholics may not accomplish that much more than people who put in shorter hours. They may take on the responsibilities of others or stretch out their own tasks in order to keep busy and preoccupied.

CHAPTER TEN

Moods

LOW SELF-ESTEEM

Although my friends tell me I'm good-looking and successful, when I look at other people, they always seem to be better-looking, smarter, and more capable than I. Why do I think this way?

You're not alone if you have these thoughts of low self-esteem. Many people feel this way to some extent. Unfortunately we're all exposed to high ideals which we can't possibly live up to. It usually begins in school and in sports, with a high level of competitiveness. You then continue to encounter them in advertising, in the movies, and on TV. The media would have us believe that the world is populated by men and women who have perfect teeth and perfect bodies, who always solve the crime, who are rich, masterful, powerful, and who always seem to make the right decision and somehow come out on top. We naturally compare ourselves with these standards of beauty and excellence, and as a result, we usually feel pretty negative about ourselves. Although we may fall somewhat short of the mark, many of us still value ourselves for what we are—rather than chastise ourselves for what we aren't.

In regard to your feelings of low self-esteem, your mind is probably playing a trick on you—it misleads you into thinking that if you were a little bit better in some physical way or more accomplished, you would feel better about yourself. This is a fallacy. If you look back to those times when you did get an A in school, or when someone told you how handsome or pretty you looked, or when the captain of the football team did ask you out, didn't you feel better for only a short period of time, if at all? Didn't you quickly revert back to your old self-deprecating mentality? I believe that external improvements won't really get to the heart of your low self-esteem. For you, this issue represents ways you came to think about yourself during your childhood. Problems of low self-esteem are central to many psychological difficulties that people have.

I admit it—I'm jealous of people who seem to have so much confidence, no matter how they do at things. How did I get to be so down on myself?

It's possible that your low self-esteem is only recent and temporary if it is tied to a major recent event such as divorce or losing a job. However, if it is pervasive and not related to a specific recent crisis in your life, we have to look further. We have to go back into your family history to find the reason that you feel so down on yourself today. For example, you may have been neglected in favor of other children. Or your parents may have been critical or had very high expectations of you. They may have been afraid that you would become lazy unless they always held the stick a little higher for you to jump over. So, to get along with your parents, you imposed their high standards upon yourself, and eventually developed feelings of worthlessness and failure.

What can I do about feeling so down on myself and alternating between jealousy of others and hopelessness?

This problem is very difficult to work on by yourself and is best treated by some form of psychotherapy. However, you could begin to work on your problem by following these steps:

1. Become aware of the problem and try to understand that you have *learned* to feel this way about yourself. Become

aware of your thinking and try to distract yourself when you catch yourself comparing and putting yourself down. Try to tune into that part of yourself that is satisfied and pleased with what you do and the way you are.

2. Realize that although you may not have the desirable attributes of others, you are in no way inferior to them as a person.

3. Be fair with yourself—give yourself a chance. When you compare yourself with others, you usually focus on their best qualities. When you see a very good-looking person, you choose to compare that person's looks to your own—not the person's intelligence; when you meet the highly intelligent person, you compare their intelligence to your own—not the person's looks. Naturally you're always coming up short, replaying the same old groove of not doing well enough, looking for ways to confirm your inferiority. This is why you feel jealous or hopeless, while someone else who is no better endowed than you does not feel the same sense of worthlessness. So when you find yourself comparing, recognize that your action is your way of putting yourself down and has little to do with the other person.

What you say makes sense and I've tried to take these steps, but it is very hard. Why is it so difficult to change this way of thinking?

The crux of the matter here is that while we say we want to change and stop comparing ourselves with others, we are also afraid to change. One factor is the myth among the people afflicted with this mentality that if we stop comparing and become more self-satisfied, we will lose our motivation to strive and achieve. In fact, the opposite is usually true. We are not productive when we feel that we have defeated ourselves. When we are more self-appreciative, we perform more and we perform better.

SADNESS AND DEPRESSION

I should be old enough and smart enough to understand myself by now, but I guess I really don't. Sometimes I seem to be sad for no reason or get overly upset over little things. For instance, yesterday my daughter broke a vase I don't even care about, and I got very sad. Is this a sign of depression?

It could be. Just because you are not aware of any reasons for your sadness or depression doesn't mean that none exists. For some people depression is a temporary state that disappears as mysteriously as it came. That doesn't change the fact that almost everyone feels mildly depressed—even miserable—at times.

Signs of serious depression that you should watch out for include feelings of persistent or severe pessimism, hopelessness, helplessness, and worry. A person who is severely depressed may appear withdrawn, indecisive, unmotivated, have trouble concentrating and remembering things, and feel a sense of self-worthlessness. There are physical signs of depression: chronic fatigue, loss of appetite and weight loss (or, for some, an increase in appetite and weight gain), sleeplessness (or sleepiness), and an inability to enjoy previously pleasurable activities, including sexual activity. Crying at the slightest thing is also a common sign. You should be aware that depression occurs in all ages, including children, adolescents, and the elderly.

Why do people get depressed? My mother says people should just look at the bright side of things.

At the root of every depression there is a loss of some kind. When this loss affects the person's own sense of his or her self-worth and hope for the future, depression occurs. Very often depression is a direct reaction to a particular event or set of life circumstances. We pretty much expect people to become somewhat depressed, for example, when they lose a job, when a marriage or other close relationship breaks up, when they become very ill, or when a child, mate, or parent dies or becomes ill. Sometimes depression occurs even when we are not aware that we are feeling worthless and hopeless.

In addition, some scientific studies indicate that there may be some biological links to depression. In other words, a person may have some inherited predisposition to being depressed, or there may be some physical cause for these feelings.

I'm a hair stylist, enjoy my work, make good money, and don't have that many problems. I meet people every day who have more problems than I do. Why am I depressed, but they're not?

When you talk about problems, I assume you mean such problems as fights with your spouse, hassles at work, a child with a minor illness, worries about paying the mortgage. These are normal, everyday problems that beset almost everyone, yet not everyone gets depressed. I think the major difference is that some people, as they were growing up, learned to connect these problems with their own self-worth; others did not.

To some extent, you probably see your problems as a reflection of your own personal failure. You blame yourself for your problems and feel that the fact that you have problems makes you worth even less. No wonder you end up feeling and acting depressed! The other people you meet may not see the same problems in their own lives as being their fault. Since they do not feel responsible for their problems, they have no reason to feel depressed.

For example, you may be having trouble at work because you are not working quickly enough. But not working quickly enough doesn't mean you are a worthless person—it only means you work slower. Meanwhile, your co-worker may be just as slow, but can accept the fact of being a slow worker and of having trouble keeping up at work. Although there may be some worries about getting fired, this person doesn't get depressed as a result of them. Loss of self-esteem, hopeless pessimism, self-hate and self-chastisement are the symptoms of depression.

My dog died two weeks ago, and people tell me I seem to be very depressed. I think I'm just sad. What is the difference between sadness and depression?

Some people feel there is no difference. But in my thinking, sadness is an emotion we all feel following a loss. It is a natural, normal lowering of our feelings. Depression involves a loss of hope and a loss of self-esteem, while sadness, in and of itself, doesn't.

I'm basically a happy person, but sometimes I feel sad or I have bad moods that come and go. Should I expect to be happy all the time? What can I do to get out of my bad moods sooner?

First, realize that though unpleasant, sadness may not always be a bad thing. In many instances it is a normal feeling, a way of adapting to and coping with a stressful life experience or loss. If you try to be "brave" or "strong" and stop yourself from giving in to an appropriate bout of sadness, or try to "snap out of it" prematurely, you may in fact be doing yourself harm. This kind of stoical behavior can result in a delayed, more chronic, and disguised expression of your feelings. So it may be wisest not to do anything but be sad under certain circumstances.

If you find yourself regularly depressed, however, some type of intervention is needed—either on your own or through psychotherapy. For example:

• *Escape and Distraction*   Many people distract themselves when they are depressed. They surround themselves with other people, go out often, or throw themselves into physical activity. For some, this seems to be helpful. However, when the depression is more severe, this type of distraction backfires. People are unable to take their minds off things, and feel worse when they try to do so.

• *Cognitive Restructuring*   This is a cognitive-behavioral technique (see Chapter Two) which involves becoming clear on the falsehoods you tell yourself that lead to your feeling a loss of self-worth. For example, you might think, "Because I lost my job, it makes me less valuable as a human being," or "Because Sally doesn't want to go out with me, no one wants to go anywhere with me." Try to catch these thoughts as they come to you; by challenging them, progress can be made.

I'm definitely depressed, but I know I could live with it. Should I see a therapist about my depression?

As you have seen, depression can be an acute, anticipated reaction that you usually overcome as you gradually learn to live with the new reality. However, depression can also be a chronic, dangerous illness. When depression becomes pervasive—progressively worse, a trap from which you see no way out—it can affect every area of your life. Not only does it reduce the quality of your life, it could shorten it. Chronic depression can ultimately lead to thoughts of self-destruction. I recommend that you seek professional help for your depression if:

• Your depression does not go away by itself or respond to the self-help measures outlined above.
• It has been going on for a long time, is very intense and/or frequent.
• Affects your ability to function socially or at work.
• You have not been able to discover what provokes it and so feel too helpless to even begin to work on it.

If I go to therapy for depression will it make me happy all the time?

I doubt that there's anything in the world that can make you happy all the time. Life is a constantly changing process of ups and downs. What psychotherapy can do is to help you try to gain some understanding of your depression, to connect with the feelings, thoughts and experiences which are repeatedly coming back to you and producing your unhappiness.

As you may have discovered, the reasons for depression are often not obvious. They may be "historical": deep-rooted, underlying conflicts that arose in your past and that have never been resolved. Usually there is also something going on in your present environment of which you may or may not be aware which triggers the depression. For example, sometimes "good" events serve as the springboard for feelings of depression. A marriage may signal the loss of independence, a child a loss of carefree couplehood, a new job the loss of the security of the old one. Even much smaller things, such as your neighbor getting a new car that you can't afford, can trigger depression. Psychotherapy may enable you to unravel the various threads that, when woven together, make up your depression.

My next-door neighbor is very depressed and is seeing a psychiatrist who wants to give her medication. How effective are the drugs prescribed for depression?

The drugs that psychiatrists prescribe to treat depression are called *antidepressant psychotropic medication*. They have been around for a number of years, and for many people they are generally effective. Occasionally it may be necessary for a psychiatrist to try more than one form of this type of medication if one does not work at first.

One of the problems with antidepressive medication is that it takes approximately two weeks to have an effect, and patients are required to take it several times a day. Since no effect is felt immediately, patients sometimes lose the motivation to keep taking the medication, which sabotages the treatment regimen.

Why would antidepressive medication be prescribed rather than using only psychotherapy?

SHOULD YOU HAVE PSYCHOTHERAPY?

As we have seen in Chapter One, some people are not amenable to psychotherapy for a myriad of reasons. Some depressed people may be interested only in getting rid of their symptoms; they take the drug, the drug helps them, and they are satisfied. In other people, the depression is so severe that they cannot benefit from psychotherapy at that time. So the therapist starts treatment with the medication, bringing the person out of the depression far enough to begin psychotherapy, which is then used in combination with the medication.

In still other situations, the depression is so severe that it threatens to disrupt a person's life. For example, a person might be so depressed as to stop going to work and thus perhaps lose a job. We turn to medication in such cases because we are looking for a relatively quick turnaround in the patient's mental state. Psychotherapy is then usually used in conjunction with medication to get at the roots of the patient's problem, to help the patient solve his problem, and to decrease the patient's dependence on the medication.

SUICIDE THOUGHTS AND ATTEMPTS

Occasionally I have momentary flashes of killing myself. For example, I sometimes think about jumping in front of an oncoming train. I know I'll never really do it, but I still wonder: am I in any danger of killing myself?

Please be reassured that this is not the way suicides usually occur. Having these thoughts occasionally is a far cry from actually committing suicide. Many people have these thoughts at times, and it doesn't in any way indicate that you are in imminent danger of killing yourself.

On the other hand, in my estimation, thoughts like these are probably an indication of either depression or guilt. You may be suppressing either or both of these feelings, so they manifest themselves as fantasies of self-destruction. If you continue to have self-destructive thoughts, however brief in duration they may be, I think it would be beneficial to talk to a therapist who can help you explore your underlying feelings so that they may be dealt with in a more direct way.

My sister sometimes calls me up in the middle of the night and talks about committing suicide. I don't know how to help her through these black moods. What can I say to her?

First of all, anyone who talks seriously about committing suicide needs professional help, and your sister seems to fit this category. Your most important job therefore is to persuade, cajole, inform, and direct your sister toward getting help for her problems.

Above and beyond that, I think it's important that you try to understand that a person who is threatening suicide is going through a major psychological crisis. This should always be taken very seriously. Sometimes your sister may try your patience, in that her view of reality seems so distorted compared to yours because she is pessimistic or very hard on herself. I urge you to be patient and understanding. Show your sister how much you love her and care about her. By doing this, you will help support her sense of self-esteem— self-esteem is certainly weakened when a person is feeling suicidal.

Above all, you should realize that you are not really equipped to fully understand nor to single-handedly save your sister from committing suicide, so don't take that burden upon yourself.

ANGER AND HOSTILITY

Sometimes my husband lashes out at me for no reason. I try to act as if nothing had happened, but I'm really hurt by this. Is this my problem or his?

It appears on the outside that since he is the angry one, it is his problem. In therapy, however, we often look upon this problem as partly belonging to both parties. With this view in mind, it's possible that you are provoking him in ways that neither of you is consciously aware of. In addition, by not telling him how much his anger hurts you, you create an environment which lets him think that this type of behavior is acceptable to you. However, there may be other factors that contribute to your husband's outbursts:

• *A Savings Account of Grievances*   It's conceivable that your husband is storing up his anger over many things you do that bother him, and then eventually exploding over a seemingly small, inconsequential issue. From your point of view, this doesn't seem to make much sense. But he feels quite justified because of the sum total of those little things.

If this is the case, you can invite your husband to explore with you the things about your behavior that have been bothering him. Ask him to talk about both those things that he has already brought up and those things he has not mentioned, perhaps because he wants to "protect" you. This is an amazing and common phenomenon: a partner pushes away complaints so as not to hurt the other person and then eventually explodes, devastating and badly hurting the mate.

In addition, be sure to let your husband know how his rages affect you in terms of your being both hurt and angry. Although having these issues out in the open may not cause them to disappear, they can be discussed and negotiated. At least your husband will be giving vent to his discontent, and his rages will probably decrease.

• *Displaced Anger*   Another possibility is that your husband is taking out his anger from other situations on you. For example, he may hate his job or his family and express his unhappiness and frustration as hostility toward you. In such situations you are the recipient of his anger because you are an easier target. Again, I suggest that you explore this with him. Try to help him come to some understanding about how he is displacing his anger upon you and how he might be able to deal with these feelings more directly.

If these measures are not successful, this should be seen as a serious problem because your bitterness toward your husband for his angry outbursts will eventually affect many areas in your relationship. I recommend that you both consider therapy either individually or as a couple.

One of my husband's best friends is extremely hostile—he thinks everything I say is wrong or stupid and tells me so. I end up never saying anything when he's around. How do I handle him? Should I be hostile back?

It sounds to me as though you have a problem with assertiveness. Clearly you are feeling angry toward this person when he puts you down and demeans you, but you are unable to express it. Assertiveness training in your particular case might consist of three possible alternatives:

1. Confront him with your feelings. Calmly tell him that you don't like it when he acts rude and hostile, that you feel put down and angry because of it.

2. If this doesn't work, I recommend that you realize how angry he is making you and then: *Get angry at him!* In this kind of situation, some people protest, "Why be angry? I can never change him." It's true that you won't change his personality, but that's not what you're really interested in. All you really want to accomplish is to change the way that he *acts* toward *you*—and if you give him a hard enough time for stepping on you, he might stop bothering you and step on someone else. In addition, by expressing your anger, you will feel better about yourself, even if you haven't affected his insufferable behavior.

3. Finally, if none of this seems to work, you might choose to avoid all contact with him. In this case, you need to *be assertive toward your husband*. Tell him that you refuse to be in this man's company, and let your husband suffer his own friends.

I'm a very easygoing, agreeable person; I almost never get angry and people tease me about it. Should I feel angry more often?

113

It's possible. However, you are the ultimate judge of what is best for you. If you are content to be the way you are, then all you need to do is to work on not being bothered by the fact that others tease you about not getting angry. Some people are simply very even-tempered and are not easily provoked.

On the other hand, bear in mind that human beings are born with an anger response. As infants, we were all designed to attack things that frustrate us or cause us pain. Infants often become angry if they are wet, or hungry, or if something gets in their way. Just watch toddlers pound or kick a chair in anger when it prevents them from getting where they want to go. As we grow up, society trains us to inhibit that angry, kicking-and-screaming response in order for us to be able to live more comfortably with each other. Imagine the world if we were all adults physically, but uninhibited one-year-olds socially. We'd have a big problem, wouldn't we? Unfortunately, this process of "socialization" sometimes goes too far. Some of us were so thoroughly taught to inhibit our anger that we don't even experience it as anger per se. I have a feeling that you have probably been taught so well to not show anger that you may not even recognize slight feelings of anger in yourself.

I pride myself on always being polite to people, even when they don't deserve it. Is it harmful to not show anger?

The cost of not experiencing anger is both interpersonal and physiological. For one thing, other people may see you as someone who doesn't get angry, and may try to take advantage of this. They may eventually dominate you and encroach more and more on your rights and territory. Other people don't have this happen to them not because they actually get angry so frequently, but rather because their associates know that they *might* get angry if they are stepped on.

In addition, there is some evidence that people who don't get outwardly angry experience the physiological components of anger just the same. By holding your anger inside, you are doing your body great harm. When you experience and express anger in some way—even if you just fantasize in your mind—the physiological components of your anger dissolve. When you don't express your anger in some way, your body takes a much longer time to bounce from the anger response back to normal. This constant stress and wear and tear may lead to hypertension, headaches, and possibly other symptoms.

What I suggest you do is to start tuning in to those situations which you see as having even the remotest possibility of getting you slightly angry. Look inside yourself to see if there's any anger there. If you don't feel the anger psychologically, see whether your body feels different. Are your muscles tighter? Does your heart beat faster? Let yourself become aware of those times when these bodily changes occur; do you also feel a glimmer of anger? I'm positive that your anger is there somewhere, but buried under years of inhibition. Therapy can be very helpful in your penetrating your own inhibition and becoming more expressive.

I'm always late—to appointments, to work, even when I'm meeting my boyfriend to see a movie. My boyfriend says that this is a sign of anger. Is he right?

It's possible, but let me begin by telling you what your problem probably is not. Some people have so many compulsive rituals about getting out of the house and are so indecisive about dressing that they end up being late for most appointments even when no one else is involved, as when they go shopping, or to a movie by themselves. In these cases, the compulsiveness and perfectionism indicated by the need to get everything just right is what slows people up to such an unbelievable degree (see Chapter Fourteen). Judging from your question, however, this compulsiveness is not at the root of your lateness problem because you mention situations that involve other people.

Your boyfriend is on the right track, but is only partially

right in his diagnosis, in the sense that anger is not the best choice of words. Mostly, chronic lateness in situations involving other people has to do with a sense of feeling out of control of these situations, and some resentment about that. You may feel that other people are setting the terms, or times, or places for your meetings. The way you express your input, power, control, and resentment in such situations is to make other people wait for you.

For example, your boyfriend may be an argumentative, controlling type of person who always insists on going to the movies he wants to see, never taking your wishes into consideration. So you are always late, as a means of exerting at least some control and of expressing some resentment. Although it is an indirect sort of communication, you find it preferable to being completely docile and going along with his wishes. If this sounds familiar, you should develop other ways to express your input. You could drop this particular boyfriend, or learn to argue and be more directly assertive. Tell him that you are put off by his always insisting on choosing the movie, and that you would like him to listen to your preferences.

However, it is not necessary for other people to actually be overly controlling or overpowering; they may just seem that way to you. Sometimes lateness has to do with an unjustified need to be in control or with feelings of resentment for some reason. For example, somewhere you may feel resentment toward your job—that you shouldn't have to work, or that you deserve a better job. One of the ways you can express your resentment is to show up late. I knew a man who was late to every single class during his entire four years in graduate school. When I asked him why he was always late, he said it was because he disliked graduate school, and particularly the professors, so much. As a result, he felt that if there was a class scheduled from 12:00 A.M. to 3:00 P.M., he owed the teacher three hours of his time and no more—including the time it took him to get to class. Consequently, he would leave his apartment at twelve o'clock and always arrive fifteen minutes late, disrupting the class and annoying the teacher. This is a perfect example of how lateness relates to the feeling of resentment at the loss of control and powerlessness, in this case in dealing with the faculty of the graduate school. Needless to say, his inability to accept the professors as they were, or to express his feelings in another way, or to come to terms with the reality of the position of a graduate student, was a detriment to his performance, grades, and relationships with his professors.

CHAPTER ELEVEN

Fears and Anxieties

WORRY, NERVOUSNESS, TENSION

I worry about everything—my job, my future, my kids. I even worry about my worrying affecting my health. Does worrying serve any purpose? Will I ever just stop worrying when things straighten out?

It does seem that worry does us no good whatsoever. Why, then, do we do so much of it? One theory is that it can be the mental equivalent of a physical flinch. Think about it: When someone goes to throw something at you or to hit you, you flinch. You shrink back and tense your muscles, and in this way your body tries to prepare you for the blow. In the same way—or so the theory goes—worry is a means of preparing you for psychological blows.

There is a certain logic to this. Imagine that you are living your life, unworried, happy, cheerful—and your family is suddenly wiped out in a car accident. Imagine what a tremendous surprise and shock you would feel. If, on the other hand, you are continually worried about your family being wiped out in a car accident, you are in essence bracing yourself psychologically against that shock. Of course, there are drawbacks to chronic worry. Most of the time our families are not wiped out in car accidents; we worry over things that are possibilities rather than probabilities. As a result, people who are frequent worriers are spending their lives in a braced position for many tragedies that will never occur. It hardly seems worth it.

You say you are a chronic worrier and wonder if you'll stop

when things "straighten out." I doubt it. Since you are a chronic worrier, your mind is actually playing a trick on you. You think: If only this situation would get solved or re-solved—if only I can keep this job, if only I can make this credit card payment, if only my daughter gets good grades—I'll never worry again! The truth of the matter is that once you are locked into the habit of worrying, there is always another worry around the corner and there is rarely any more than temporary relief.

But surely there are reasons to be concerned about some things in life?

Yes, there are, but there's a difference between worrying and constructive concern. Worry tends to be *unproductive, obsessive,* and *repetitive*. We worry about many things we can't do anything about. It is ironic that worry often backfires on us and causes stress and creates some of the things we worry about, such as ill health.

On the other hand, when you are concerned, you hold back and deliberately examine something before you decide to go ahead with it. Occasionally we may stop and decide not to go ahead. Even so, if our thinking leads to some sense of action or conclusion, this is productive concern, not worry.

Why is it so hard to stop worrying? What can I do to stop?

You probably learned to worry from your parents, and have been unable to break this habit of worry because you are afraid to stop. Worriers like you have been trained to believe that if they relax and let things happen, that first of all, the very catastrophe they are worrying about will be brought on and that second, they will be caught off guard. As a worrier, you feel it's best to be tense and be prepared for the worst.

I definitely recommend that you try to curb your worrying habit. Many scientific studies have shown that worry causes stress—wear and tear on the body. Here are the steps you might want to take:

1. Buy one or more of the many books about stress and relaxation which present relaxation exercises to do on your own. These may give you some relief, if you do them regularly.

2. Biofeedback training is another approach to relaxation that works for many people. Consult with a professional who has biofeedback expertise.

3. Become more acutely aware of yourself worrying and allow yourself to relax, or try to distract yourself.

4. When your worry is about one or two topics and has a driven flavor to it, behavioral psychotherapy may give you some techniques for stopping it, such as the behavioral technique called "thought stopping." In this technique, you yell the word "STOP" either out loud or just to yourself mentally. This disrupts the chain of worry temporarily, which you then disrupt again by repeating the word "stop." If the worry persists, your therapist may suggest that you wear a rubber band around your wrist. By snapping the rubber band every time you say "stop," the pain serves to further disrupt severe worrying patterns. Eventually the word "stop" becomes forceful enough to stop the pattern without your using the rubber band.

5. Psychotherapy in general may help you unravel the worry component in your personality.

People are always telling me that I'm very tense, that I should learn to relax. But I don't notice it. Should I listen to them?

You should listen to them because these people are probably right about your tension. Other people can often see some body tension in you of which you are unaware. It's not uncommon for people to be unaware of how tense they are because they've become used to it. A fish doesn't realize it's in water, either.

You might try some kind of relaxation, such as meditation or biofeedback, to give you some sense of being in another state and so enable you to see what the difference is. If you do notice a difference, continuing with these practices will be of benefit.

A relaxation technique you might like to try on your own is called *Progressive Relaxation*. To practice this technique, you begin by sitting or lying in a comfortable position, preferably in a quiet, darkened room. You then alternately tense and relax individual muscle groups in your body. Beginning with your feet, work up each leg, tensing and then relaxing your calves, thighs, and buttocks. Then work on your torso, your shoulders, your hands and arms, neck, head, and face. Books and audio tapes that teach you this technique are widely available, and many people have found them to be very helpful.

I know I'm very tense, but how can I be otherwise considering my high-pressure job, my precarious financial situation, and my helpless, overly demanding husband?

Yes, it does sound as if you have a high share of stressful situations in your life. Many other people in your position would also feel justified in feeling anxious and tense. However, not everyone is equally stressed by the same situations. So I don't think you should simply write off your reactions to things by relying on the excuse that things are tough for you. It is my belief that most people can find some concrete ways to reduce the load that they are carrying.

• *Lighten Your Load* Many people who feel as stressed as you sound believe they have to take responsibility for a tremendous number of things. This acute sense of responsibility and indispensability lets other people off the hook and leaves you on it. This sets up a vicious cycle: The boss knows you can never say no, so he always asks you first. And since you can never say no, you take on more and more. Consider the ways you can say no, or start saying no in your head, and take on fewer responsibilities in your family, at work, and with friends.

• *Be Realistic* In addition, you may exaggerate the consequences of things not going well, and so tackle the responsibilities you do have in an obsessive way. Some of the stress you feel may come from within yourself. Cognitive behavior therapy—learning how to rethink these situations—as well as the relaxation techniques mentioned earlier may help. Other types of psychotherapies may help to get at the roots of these stressful thinking habits.

INSOMNIA

I can't seem to fall asleep at night, and sometimes when I finally do, I wake up much too early and can't fall back asleep. Should I take sleeping pills?

Sleeping pills are usually not the answer to insomnia. You can grow dependent on pills, so it is unwise to take them more than one or two nights in a row. In addition, they can cause some undesirable side effects such as a disturbed sleep/dream pattern at night and a groggy feeling the next day.

It is better to try to get at the root of your problem—*why* can't you sleep? Insomnia—the frequent or chronic inability to sleep—is often due to anxiety. However, it can also stem from other emotional difficulties, such as depression. In addition, once you develop a pattern of not being able to sleep, you tend to worry about not being able to sleep, which just adds to your difficulties. To solve your insomnia problem, there are a number of steps you can take:

1. You might want to look for a Sleep Center. These are located in some large cities, and they specialize in the treatment of sleep disorders. They teach you how to use relaxation and biofeedback techniques that are often helpful to insomniacs.

2. If your sleep problem is an expression of a wider-ranging problem, such as anxiety or depression, you should con-

sider psychotherapy. A behavioral psychotherapist might be helpful for a direct approach to the problem.

3. Get one of the several self-help books available, which suggest regimens to help you sleep. Some of these include, for example:

- Have a set time to go to bed and get out of bed for the day eight hours later, regardless of how much you've slept.
- Under no circumstances, take naps during the day.
- If you don't fall asleep, or you wake up and don't fall back asleep within a brief period of time, don't lie in bed trying to sleep; rather, get up and perform some boring task for at least half an hour. If, after this period, you go back to bed and after another half hour are still not able to fall asleep, get up again and repeat the boring task.

The purpose of this program is to break the habit of lying in bed and "trying to sleep," which contributes to insomnia. It also creates a state where the body will need sleep so badly that it will override the tension that is keeping you awake.

FEARS, PHOBIAS, AND PANIC ATTACKS

I have a friend who is unbelievably afraid of all dogs. He won't even go near small puppies, and he quickly turns the page of a magazine that has a picture of a dog on it. I admit I get a little nervous and fearful around big dogs that look dangerous. I wonder if I have a phobia—what's the difference between phobia and fear?

All fears are not phobias. Sometimes fears are reasonable and based on good sense. For example, you are probably wise to be afraid when you see a large, unleashed barking dog. You would also not be phobic if you were reluctant to climb up a rickety ladder. These situations could actually hurt you, so your fears are self-preserving. They won't "spread" or disable or preoccupy you.

Phobias, on the other hand, are reactions that are exaggerations of the probability or severity of danger. A phobia is an intense, irrational, uncontrollable and sometimes disabling fear that causes you to avoid whatever objects, situations, or people are responsible for setting off this response. I would therefore say that your friend is phobic. A person who is phobic of dogs is usually "terrified" of all dogs—even tiny ones—and may walk across the street or hesitate to go out if there is a possibility of even seeing a dog. Fear of flying is another example of exaggerating the probability that something negative will happen. None of us wants to be in a plane crash, but we fly anyway because we think the probability of such a mishap is very small; one explanation for a person being phobic of flying is that he or she exaggerates the probability that the plane will crash, and so of course can never fly.

What are the most common fears and phobias?

Some of the common phobias are:
  acrophobia, an abnormal fear of heights
  aerophobia, a fear of air, which includes flying in planes, and of drafts
  agoraphobia, fear of open spaces, crowds, traveling
  ailurophobia, fear of cats
  claustrophobia, fear of enclosed spaces
  pyrophobia, fear of fire
  thanatophobia, fear of death
  xenophobia, fear of things and people that are strange or foreign
  zoophobia, fear of animals

Why are phobias so hard to get rid of?

The answer to this question varies, depending upon the orientation of the therapist. If you ask an analytically oriented therapist, he or she will tell you that although a phobia may look like a relatively simple problem—for example, you are afraid of enclosed places, so you don't go into elevators—in the analyst's mind it is not a simple problem at all. It is really a symbolic representation of a deep-rooted early childhood problem. Unless you can recognize and work out this child-hood problem, you will not be rid of your phobia.

The more direct behavioral approach differs in that it attempts to deal directly with the symptom. Phobias almost always involve avoidance of a situation or object. As long as you continue to avoid that situation or object, you are going to continue to be afraid of it. Behavioral therapists have recognized that people who are phobic are sometimes very much afraid of becoming afraid. As a result, it is sometimes very difficult to get people to attempt to take even small steps toward a phobic situation or object because this causes them to experience small amounts of fear.

Finally, behaviorists also take into consideration that once a phobia is established in a person's life, there may be certain payoffs that he or she is unwilling to give up. For example, if the person is afraid of going out alone, this may insure that members of the patient's family will meet their so-called responsibility to be traveling companions for the patient. Phobias also give people a sense of control over their environment and over people around them. These patterns of interpersonal interactions around the phobia are sometimes very difficult to dislodge.

I get very nervous and tongue-tied at big parties with unfamiliar people, when I have to face my boss, or make a speech or presentation. Would it work if I took a couple of tranquilizers to calm me down?

You may find it reassuring to know that public speaking is the most common fear in America. The tranquilizers may help, but they may also make you drowsy, which would hinder your performance. It might be more helpful to accept the fact that you are afraid and to plunge ahead. Sometimes people are more afraid in the anticipation of these speeches and talks than in the actuality. Let me also reassure you that the more presentations you do, the better—with each experience, your fear will lessen.

If the fear of public speaking really bothers you and the ability to do it is very important to you, therapy can help. The behavioral approach offers short-term therapies which have been particularly successful with this problem. In addition, there are courses, classes, and groups that focus on public speaking. Again, they rely mainly on behavioral techniques, along with group support, to help you overcome these fears. This may be the most economical and effective way to begin to deal with this problem.

I have a phobia of flying and it really bothers me how much this limits my life, but I'm too ashamed to talk about it. What kind of help can therapy give me?

Phobics often believe that they are alone in their fears. Many are unable to explain why they are afraid, and they are ashamed to discuss the problem with anyone, sometimes even a doctor. But you should not feel ashamed, alone, or hopeless about your fear of flying. Many other people experience this same fearfulness.

Behaviorists often treat phobias and have worked quite successfully with your type of problem in attempting to directly reduce the fear. One approach acclimates you to flying gradually with positive results, often beginning with asking you to imagine the experience of flying. Another approach exposes you to the actual experience of flying by having you first go to the airport, then meet the crew and enter the plane, then taxi down the runway, and finally actually fly. One form of therapy, called implosion therapy, gets you to experience the fear intensely, fully, for a prolonged period of time. This is based on the notion that when we are *fully* exposed to anything fear-evoking for a long enough period of time, the fear will decrease. Hypnosis and relaxation techniques are sometimes helpful. There are also special groups and courses offered in large cities that are specifically oriented toward people with a fear of flying. Most therapists treat patients that are suffering from phobias. However, they approach the problem from a less specific, more generalized, therapy point of view. I believe that if the direct methods are not successful, then the more generalized approaches should be considered.

I find I'm going out of the house less and less. I tend to be more comfortable at home, with my family. Am I developing a phobia of going out?

This certainly is one of the ways that people develop a pattern of not leaving home because of their fear of going out. Over a period of time, a person comes to feel more and more nervous and uneasy at being outside. Eventually the individual reaches the point of giving up socializing entirely. Sometimes, though, this pattern develops in a more dramatic way, where the person has an acute anxiety attack—pounding heart, dizziness, difficulty breathing—and from then on rarely goes out of the house. This fear is called *agoraphobia;* it afflicts women more often than it does men, and can last for years.

I was mugged recently and for days afterward I was so afraid I had to force myself to go out of the house. I'm better now, but did I have agoraphobia? What causes these feelings of panic at the idea of going out?

No—not really. Although you were afraid to go out, your fear was normal given your past experience. I think most people would be afraid to go out after being mugged—for a while at least. The important thing, however, is that this fear gradually dissipated and you were functioning again. If you were truly agoraphobic, this wouldn't happen very easily. Agoraphobia refers to a behavior pattern that is chronic. Agoraphobia can be *triggered* by a traumatic event such as being burglarized or mugged. In such instances, the person involved is very fearful to begin with. As a result of an overall fearful mentality, the person cannot seem to shake this fear after a traumatic event occurs.

In other people, it sometimes develops as a means of expressing dependency, or of controlling other family members when the agoraphobic feels powerless to do so in the ordinary way. Another notion is that this syndrome is a wife's unconscious attempt to restrain herself from leaving her husband. The woman is caught in an intense conflict between breaking up or staying together: too afraid to go out on her own, too miserable not to.

I once treated a woman who had not gone out of the house for seventeen years. In this case, the agoraphobia developed because of the husband's incessant jealousy. He would call her four or five times a day and, if she wasn't at home, he would reprimand her. So she started going out less and less, and eventually she didn't go out at all. It was as if she was saying to him, "Okay; you want to make sure I'm not running around? I'll show you—I'll *really* stay home." This husband later tried to encourage his wife to leave the house; however, she was too phobic to do so.

Several times over the last six months I've gotten panic attacks, where I just don't know what to do. Will they ever go away?

There's no guarantee that they will. Usually, when people begin to experience panic attacks, there is something in their life that is frightening them which they are refusing to recognize. Although they usually deny the frightening thought whenever it comes into their heads, they can't block out the physical component of their fear. It has to come out somewhere, and in this case it has become manifest as a racing heart, tight muscles, and sweating palms.

For example, I have a patient who is facing two difficult things in her life. She is beginning to recognize her anger at her mother and at her husband, both of whom are very domineering. She's trying to deny her anger because it is very scary to her. As she starts to feel her anger, it frightens her so much that she experiences panic instead, and so she barely recognizes the anger that is setting off the panic.

How is agoraphobia treated?

Anyone who is experiencing worsening symptoms of a fear of going out of the house should seek professional help before these avoidance patterns become more entrenched. This problem can escalate rather quickly. Psychotherapy traditionally utilizes behavior modification, confrontation, and relaxation techniques such as hypnosis; psychoanalytic approaches work on the underlying mentality involved with the problem. In addition, some doctors have been able to bring panic attacks under control by using drugs.

CHAPTER TWELVE

Destructive Problem Habits

OVEREATING AND OTHER EATING DISORDERS

It seems like I've been overweight all my life. I'd really like to lose thirty pounds. I've been on every diet in the world. Why can't I lose weight?

Unless there is something wrong with you physically—and I urge you to get a thorough medical exam to rule this out—the reason you haven't been able to lose weight seems simple. Although you say you've been on many diets, you probably haven't been able to *stay* on any of them long enough to reach and maintain the weight you desire. There are many people who have gotten a diet that is appropriate for them—from a book or a magazine or a friend, but usually they get it from a physician or dietician. They have successfully followed the diet, and lost weight. With careful monitoring, most of the lost weight has stayed off. For some people, losing weight is that simple.

However, many others, like yourself, for whatever reason, cannot follow a diet and lose weight on their own. When that is the case, I have two suggestions to offer:

1. *Join a weight-loss group* This approach supplies group guidance, encouragement, and support, some general insights into the psychological aspects of the problem, and some pressure and motivation to lose weight. Many people with chronic weight problems have been helped by these groups. Weight Watchers has been highly successful and is perhaps the best-known, but there are many groups available. Their styles and focuses vary somewhat, so it pays to try out

a few in order to find the one that appeals to you most.

2. *Go for specialized psychotherapy* If you find the support group approach, too, is unsuccessful, you may want to enter an individual or group psychotherapy program with someone who has expertise in eating disorders. Your therapist will help you find out why you have been resistant to losing weight and what in particular in your life is interfering with your efforts to stay on a diet. It is possible that members of your family may be consciously or unconsciously interfering with your attempt to lose weight, and your psychotherapist will help you look into this possibility.

I really don't understand—of course I want to lose weight. Why would I self-sabotage my dieting efforts?

Overweight has many possible psychological underpinnings; it is not just a matter of using your "will power" to eat less.

These are just some of the basic reasons that losing weight is not a simple, easy matter for some people, and why psychotherapy may be needed to deal with it:

• *Fear of Being Thin* If you are actually afraid to be thin, you use your fatness as a defense and an excuse for many things you don't want to face. You may say, "I can't play sports, get promoted, or be popular because I'm too heavy." In actuality, you may unconsciously fear that you are basically incompetent or unlikable.

• *Fear of Sexuality and Sex* Some people use their fatness as a way of denying their sexuality or of avoiding sex. Instead of accepting the fact that you are a sexual being by acting upon your sexual desires or at least considering how these desires may be affecting your interaction with others, you may be making yourself overweight to deny your sexual self or to avoid sex. Since fat is considered unattractive by today's society, you may be putting on weight so that others will not find you sexually desirable; if you are not desirable as a potential sex partner, you do not have to engage in sex. Also, by making yourself unattractive, you may be trying to hide the fact that you are interested in sex—both from others and from yourself.

• *A Poor Self-Image* Sometimes people really dislike themselves deep down, and they stay fat in order to punish themselves. Perhaps your self-image is that of an overweight, unattractive, unappealing person. By staying fat, you confirm this image of yourself.

I hate being fat—I really do want to lose weight, and much of the time I don't even think about food. But whenever I feel depressed or anxious, I find myself eating second and third helpings of everything. Why do I only overeat when things aren't going right?

This brings up another possible reason why many people have trouble with their weight: appetite control. Very often people cannot control their eating because they are depressed or feel sorry for themselves, and eating makes them feel better temporarily. Maybe you feel at times that life is so hard, times are so tough, and things are so bad for you, why should you deprive yourself of anything more? Overeating, particularly binge eating, is frequently a way of dealing with anxiety: food distracts and calms you, but unfortunately it doesn't directly confront your anxiety and so it doesn't solve the problem. Some form of psychotherapy is needed to help you deal directly with whatever is bothering you and making you tense and anxious.

I've successfully lost the twenty pounds I wanted to, but I'm afraid I'll gain it back because I'm still obsessed by food. How can I keep from gaining it back?

It's understandable that if you've recently lost the weight, you're going to be concerned that you'll gain it back. This concern may naturally diminish with time.

However, whether you keep the weight off or not depends to a great extent on how you lost it in the first place. If you've lost the weight by crash dieting and/or frantic exercise and you are now going back to your normal eating habits and lifestyle, you probably *will* gain it back. Since successful weight loss involves a more permanent change in your eating and exercise habits, the more you focus on establishing a routine of eating and exercise that you can live with over the long haul, the more stable your weight will become.

Once you have established an effective maintenance routine, you can take some of the psychological pressure off yourself. Although you may have to be aware of your weight and to "behave" to a certain degree for the rest of your life, you needn't be obsessive about it forever. Eventually you will be able to reach the point where you can adopt a more relaxed attitude toward attaining and maintaining the "perfect" weight. If you do at some point see yourself beginning to gain again, don't panic—simply check it before it gets out of hand.

Although I normally eat very little at mealtimes, I sometimes go on terrible binges and stuff myself uncontrollably on potato chips and peanuts while I'm alone. Am I right to worry?

Worry won't do any good, but what you might do is try to figure out what the binges are all about. Any number of motivating factors can be at work here. As previously mentioned, sometimes food can be used to stave off feelings of anxiety or depression. The fact that these binges occur when you are alone indicates that most likely you have some suppressed thoughts and feelings which threaten to come to the surface when you are not distracted by the company of other people. My recommendation is that you enter some kind of therapy to work out this problem before it gets worse. There are therapists who specialize in eating disorders of this type.

I've been hearing about these young girls—some of them quite famous—who gorge themselves on food. Since they're still thin, how can bingeing be dangerous?

In the extreme, food bingeing is frequently followed by purging, in which the person induces vomiting afterward. This condition is called *bulimia*. Bulimia may also accompany *anorexia,* a lack of desire to eat leading to self-starvation. Anorexia and bulimia are most common among young women, but men may suffer too. Both of these disorders can be very dangerous to the body and may lead to death. They should be treated by a professional without delay. Special therapy programs, conducted by teams of physicians, psychologists, and nutritionists, are available in some hospitals. There are also self-help groups which may prove useful.

My ten-year-old is overweight for his height. His friends tease him about it, and I know it hurts him, but he still eats everything in sight. What can I do?

There is much that you can do to help your son, or anyone else you care about who has a weight problem. You can begin by providing him with healthful, low-calorie meals. *Don't nag!* Harping on the problem will probably only serve to make him eat more to assert his independence, or as a comfort for being reprimanded. Do your best to encourage exercise and interests to take the place of food.

When a growing child is overweight, many experts suggest that the best approach is not one of getting him to *lose weight,* but one of getting him to *stop gaining.* As his height increases, he will grow into his weight. In addition, it may be helpful if you do some examining of your own motives and actions in allowing your son to become overweight in the first place. What kind of example are you setting? Are you overweight? What kinds of foods do you eat? Do you get any exercise? Obesity does tend to run in families, and the menus and eating habits he has been growing up with may be partly responsible for his problem now.

SMOKING

What's the best way to stop smoking? I've been smoking for eight years. I've tried and tried, but I just can't seem to kick the habit.

There is no one magical way that works for everyone. Although some people manage to quit on their own, there are many organizations, health institutions, and health professionals that conduct programs that may prove helpful. Popular and successful programs include the SmokEnders' program, the Seventh Day Adventists' program, and the American Cancer Society's free Quit Smoking Clinics.

These groups will provide you with information, an environment that stimulates questions and discussion, and some specific techniques and exercises such as role-playing and relaxation exercises. Some people also seem to benefit from hypnosis, wherein the therapist plants a suggestion in your mind that you will be able to stop smoking. In some cases, therapists use aversion therapy as well. In one type of aversion therapy, you smoke a great number of cigarettes rapidly without stopping until you become nauseated.

All techniques employed to stop smoking require some degree of motivation. It is important to realize that you cannot go into these programs expecting the personnel to make you want to stop. You must first reach the decision to stop on your own; these programs then serve to support and boost that decision.

ALCOHOLISM

I really enjoy drinking. It makes my day go faster. But my friends are concerned that I'm becoming an alcoholic. Are they right to be concerned?

Whether or not you are an alcoholic depends upon how much you're drinking and what purpose alcohol serves in your life.

Rather than drinking socially, you seem to be using alcohol as a drug to relieve boredom or discomfort, perhaps at home, perhaps on the job. In my opinion, if you are not an alcoholic now, you are certainly on the road to becoming one. I hope you can begin to realize that the alcohol will not really solve your problems. It will probably make them worse or add new problems which are then usually covered up by the further use of alcohol.

I don't drink much during the week. But over the weekends I polish off a quart of vodka, all by myself. What can I do about this?

You definitely have a drinking problem. For you, as for all alcoholics, the first step in overcoming this problem is your ability to acknowledge that it exists and that you need help. Alcoholics Anonymous is helpful to many people. It is group-oriented (and spiritually oriented) and consists of re-covering alcoholics who gain strength through sharing experiences and struggles with other members at regular meetings. If this sounds like it's for you, I recommend it. If not, there are also other organizations which offer self-help alcohol programs that have different approaches to the problem.

In addition, psychotherapy is often helpful in treating alco-holism. Therapy addresses the problem in a somewhat dif-ferent way and will attempt to work through with you some of the underlying causes of your turning to alcohol, to increase your self-awareness, and to change self-destructive behavior. There are also drugs available which either deter drinking by causing unpleasant side effects, or which alleviate severe withdrawal symptoms that sometimes accompany detoxifica-tion. Many health insurance policies cover the expense of treatment for alcoholism. So there are several choices, and no matter which one you choose, it will be a step in the right direction.

My husband denies it, but I think he's an alcoholic. He has blackouts and sometimes can't get up to go to work. What can I do to help him and to help myself deal with it?

Your husband is using denial, which is a very common stage in alcoholism. But like all alcoholics, your husband's drinking is symptomatic of other problems, and he is using alcohol in an attempt to deal with these problems. Bearing this in mind, try to become supportive and understanding and to create the kind of environment in which he can really discuss his problems and his alcoholism with you—not an environment in which you are accusatory or outraged, but one in which you recognize his suffering. Because of your support and communication, he might turn toward one of the treatments mentioned earlier.

For yourself and your family, there are self-help groups for people who are relatives of alcoholics. One of them is called Al-Anon, which is associated with Alcoholics Anonymous. The members are relatives of alcoholics just like you, and their support and counseling will definitely be helpful to you.

How do you know when a person is an alcoholic?

I must admit that the exact definition is somewhat in dispute. However, some of the indications are thought to be:
- When alcohol is destructive to the person's life and/or body.
- When alcohol is *needed* rather than chosen.
- When alcohol is used to cover up or cope with a problem, rather than as a means of socializing.

Specific signs might include:
- Making excuses to drink.
- Drinking surreptitiously or otherwise lying about drinking habits.
- Drinking in the morning.
- Having blackouts.
- Maintaining poor eating habits.
- Taking drinks to "relax."

My father was an alcoholic and I'm worried that I might follow in his footsteps. What causes some people to become alcoholics but not others?

Although some authorities claim that there may be underlying physical causes of alcoholism, there is no conclusive scientific evidence either for this or for the theory that alcoholism is inherited. However, it does appear that people, through any number of psychological mechanisms—following a role model, parental training, negative self-esteem, anxiety—*do* sometimes follow in a mother's or father's footsteps and end up using alcohol to solve their problems. Just because you have an alcoholic father, you should not assume that you will become an alcoholic. However, if you begin to recognize in yourself any of the signs listed above, you should be as concerned as anyone else would be.

DRUGS

My daughter has been acting strangely lately, and I don't really approve of the new group of friends she's been hanging out with. How do I know whether they're using drugs?

To the untrained eye, it may be difficult to detect drug abuse in the early stages. But any of the following may indicate a drug problem in your daughter or in her friends: change in friends, lack of motivation, abrupt mood swings, red eyes or dilated pupils, change in sleeping habits, weight change, secrecy, or a change in personal hygiene.

I suspect that my teen-age son is a drug addict. What should I do if he is?

If your son is dependent on drugs, you should certainly confront him with whatever evidence you have. My belief is that you must persuade, convince him—or coerce him if necessary—to seek treatment. You should not provide an environment which psychologically or financially supports his addiction. Giving in to a drug addict, pleading with him to make promises he is physically and psychologically unable to keep, overlooking the problem, or hoping that it will stop—these are actions that almost always prove fruitless and ultimately destructive. You really must be very strong and create a situation where he has no alternative other than to get treatment.

You must also realize that physical addiction to drugs is only a part of your son's problem. Drugs have drawn him into a social group bound together by mutual dependency and common status as outlaws. Treatment for drug addiction is not only a matter of undergoing and maintaining detoxification. It must also be able to provide alternative interests that are as all-consuming as the former lifestyle of the drug addict, and a social and psychological existence that is at least as satisfying.

Sometimes I'm so nervous and anxious I just need to take a tranquilizer to calm me down. Does this mean I might become dependent on the drugs I'm taking?

Let me begin by asking you what you mean by the word "need"? What would happen if you didn't have drugs to calm you down? You would remain anxious for a while, but eventually you would become less anxious. So your "need" is one that is created by the availability of the drug. Yes, you might become dependent on the drug. All of these drugs, because they do provide immediate relief, eventually create a sense of psychological dependency. You always run the risk of starting to take the drug sooner and sooner, in larger and larger doses, to relieve smaller and smaller amounts of anxiety. That's where the danger is. If you take something to help you relax temporarily in a crisis situation, that's one thing. But if drugs become a regular part of your lifestyle as a means of coping with the world around you, that's another. Think about it the next time you feel the "need" to pop a pill: Drugs usually are not a very good long-term solution because you can become dependent on them, and they do not resolve the real problems.

I know I'm addicted to drugs. Is it possible to kick a drug habit on your own?

Yes, anything is possible. However, experience has shown that most people have a very hard time kicking drugs on their own. Many are able to stop for a while, during a slack period. But as soon as whatever made them turn to drugs in the first place presents itself again, they return to drugs. So if you do try to kick your drug habit on your own, but find that you are still troubled, be honest with yourself and get some help.

What kind of treatment is there for drug addiction? I'm afraid I won't be able to ask for help without getting in trouble with the police.

First of all, let me reassure you that patient records must be kept confidential, so don't let your fear of the law keep you from seeking the help you need.

Both outpatient and inpatient treatment is available for drug abuse. However, if you are really dependent on drugs, as opposed to being an occasional or even frequent user, outpatient treatment usually is not recommended because it is too difficult to stay off drugs as an outpatient. You will probably find that entering some sort of inpatient drug-addict rehabilitation is more successful. During the first part of the treatment you will live at the facility, but gradually you will grow more capable of being out on your own. You may locate drug abuse clinics by calling your city, county, or state mental health organization, or a university hospital. Many of these clinics are government-funded and either are free or have sliding-scale fees.

CHAPTER THIRTEEN

Sexual Problems

INHIBITION AND LACK OF DESIRE

We've been happily married for five years, but our desire to make love is less than it was during the first year or so. Is this normal?

Yes, unless the decline has been substantial and rapid. After the initial state of passion is played out, sexual interest often decreases somewhat on the part of one or both partners. However, desire also depends upon your age, your physical health, and your gender. Men's desires often decrease with age, while women usually experience an increase up until their middle years, which is followed by a decrease. Your lack of desire is a problem only if you and your husband are out of sync—that is, if one partner's desire wanes more than the other's—or if one or both of you is distressed by the downswing in physical intimacy.

My husband is concerned because he wants to have sex more often than I do. In fact, lately I don't want to have sex at all. I'm afraid that this is going to ruin our marriage. What can I do?

This situation sounds as if there is more than a simple fading of desire. There may be a number of possible reasons for this dis-synchronization of sexual desire:

• *Unfulfilled Desires* You may feel that you are not getting what you want sexually. Perhaps you have become bored or dissatisfied with the sex act itself, but are unable to tune in to exactly what is wrong about it for you. I suggest that you explore this possibility with your husband. Although it may be difficult for you at first, try to talk to him openly and

141

honestly. It has always amazed me that people can be married for many, many years, and still be reluctant to candidly express their sexual desires. But talking it out calmly, without blaming anyone, may allow you to express yourself sexually in a more interesting and exciting way.

• *Other Problems*   Another possibility to consider is that something else, such as worry or depression, is interfering with your ability to freely experience eroticism. If this is the case, your best course of action is to deal with these larger problems and see if your sexual problems also improve.

• *Sex as a Scapegoat*   Third, although you say you are happily married, your marriage may not be running quite as smoothly as you believe. I have found that when sex has become an issue between a couple—when one feels coerced or dominated by the other or in some way feels resentful— that person tends to unconsciously turn off sexually toward the other. This may be happening to you, even though you may not fully experience resentment toward your husband. If you are denying your anger from moment to moment, you may want to explore this possibility either within your own mind or between you and your husband.

Like most behavior, sexual desire varies in most people. But if this change persists for more than a month or so, there is probably something going on here that you may want to look into further, either with a sex therapist or counselor or a broader-based psychotherapist.

Some of the men I date put a lot of pressure on me to have sex with them, but it just seems wrong to me. Am I frigid?

I wonder if the men you are saying no to are telling you you're frigid in order to coerce you into having sex with them. Don't let them browbeat you or frighten you into saying yes. Tune in to your own feelings. It's important that you follow your intuition about whom you would feel comfortable and confident being intimate with. Choosing not to have sex with someone whom you're not comfortable with or whom you are not attracted to has nothing to do with being frigid—it's just good common sense. People often say that a woman is frigid only if she habitually experiences either no desire or a limited sexual desire, or she actually does have sex but just goes through the motions. I see nothing in your question that implies that you have this problem.

Although I like sex very much, I've never been able to have an orgasm. Is there any hope for me?

Yes, there is. Assuming there is no medical reason for your inability to achieve orgasm (and if you haven't gone to a medical doctor about this, I strongly urge you to do so), you probably have a problem with inhibition. Although you may not think that you are sexually inhibited, our society has always had a great deal of inhibition in this area, and as a result, most of us have been brought up to be inhibited in some way. Even though you may not remember being trained in antisexual ways because the training takes place so early and is so subtle, it is there. It is also possible that you are not getting the appropriate physical stimulation to achieve orgasm. Either you have inadequately explored the possibilities, or you are too shy to really tell or show your partners what you like.

I recommend that you go to a sex therapist who will explore this problem with you. If you have a steady partner, it is sometimes helpful to work together on this. There *is* hope, especially since you say you basically enjoy sex.

SEX AND PARENTHOOD

Since our baby was born six months ago, our sex life has been practically nonexistent. We don't even cuddle the way we used to. How can we get our relationship back on the right track?

As you are experiencing firsthand, the addition of a new baby can wreak havoc with the relationship between the parents. It is quite normal for new mothers to experience a lowered sex drive because of altered hormone levels, the stress and anxiety surrounding motherhood, and sheer exhaustion. There is not much you can do about the hormone levels, but there are other steps you can take to correct the situation.

1. As parents, you can try to share the tasks involved in child care. In addition, look at ways that you can transfer some of the work to someone else—shere tasks with neighbors, ask relatives to baby-sit, have things delivered. You need a break some of the time.

2. Examine whether your anxiety over your new role and responsibilities as a parent is taking its toll on your sexual desire. It is all too easy to become too involved with the needs and charms of the baby, at the expense of your spouse.

3. Reconnect with each other—realize your relationship with your husband will never be exactly the same as when there were just the two of you, but that the baby can bring you closer, and ultimately you can improve upon what you had.

4. If you miss the cuddling, begin physical intimacy with that—it doesn't take much energy, and can go a long way in reestablishing the emotional and physical bond between you. Gradually broaden your expression of affection and sensuality, until you have resumed lovemaking and enjoy a more fulfilling sexual relationship.

I'm very concerned that our children are going to walk in on us while we're in the middle of making love. It's inhibiting us in bed—how concerned should we be and how do we handle it if one of them does walk in?

My first suggestion to you is to take the practical step of telling your children not to come in without knocking or when there's a "Do Not Disturb" sign on the door. This should help put you at ease.

If, however, your children do walk in, remember that although it may be embarrassing, it is not necessarily damaging to the children if you don't become visibly upset or angry or offer no explanation. Ask your children what they think is happening. Then explain that what you and your spouse are doing is enjoyable and that this is one way that adults play and show their love for each other. If your children ask to join in, say that they will have to wait until they are grown up and have found someone they love the same way you love your spouse.

PREMATURE EJACULATION AND IMPOTENCE

I suffer from premature ejaculation. How common is this? It's ruining my sex life.

It is fairly common, but that doesn't improve your situation. Anyone with this problem should first go for a medical exam to rule out any physical problems.

If no physical cause can be found, your premature ejaculation may be caused by anxiety or tension about performing during sex. If you are nervous about your sexual performance, it is likely that you have gotten yourself into a vicious cycle; your experiencing this problem *causes* your anxiety and tension, and this anxiety and tension in turn cause your physical problem to occur—again and again. That is why it is very common to hear people complaining of this problem getting worse and worse.

In terms of treatment, I recommend going to a professional, especially one who specializes in behavioral therapy and sex therapy. This type of therapy for your problem tends to be fairly short-term and very successful. Masters and Johnson have come up with a technique called "the squeeze," whereby the penis is desensitized so that your tendency toward premature ejaculation is reduced, thus restoring your confidence. Other behavioral techniques that your therapist may prescribe involve inserting the penis without very much movement initially, along with timing schedules which gradually increase the amount of stimulation without reaching orgasm. Of course, there are also other, long-term approaches—such as psychoanalysis—which explore the underlying reasons for the anxiety surrounding sexual intercourse and performance.

I've heard that most impotence results from physical causes. Is that true?

Although impotence sometimes has biological causes, most often it does not. There are two varieties of impotence:

Primary impotence occurs when a man cannot perform sexually in any situation.

Secondary impotence occurs under certain circumstances only. For example, a man may be able to masturbate or have sex with one partner in particular, but he may be impotent with another partner or the first time sex occurs with a new partner.

While primary impotence does occasionally have physical causes, secondary impotence is clearly psychological in origin.

PROMISCUITY

I have a friend who goes from man to man without ever finding anyone with whom she is happy. I sometimes feel she's being used by them. What's wrong with her?

Why are you so quick to assume that something is wrong with your friend? Would you feel the same way if your friend were a man who went from woman to woman? Women are still unfairly condemned for having many men, and perhaps you should ask yourself whether you aren't applying a double standard to the situation. It's possible that your friend is happy in her lifestyle although you might not be.

Aside from that, we need to consider whether your friend would rather be monogamous and is somehow unable to be so. Is she going from man to man in a compulsive, driven way? If so, it raises many issues. One possibility is that she is really trying to avoid staying with one person because she finds intimacy or commitment threatening. Another possibility is that she needs to be reassured that she is attractive, or loved, or capable of making conquests. Most compulsive behavior doesn't lead to happiness. Your friend may have this driving need to seduce the next man, but the assurance she gets is short-lived and must be constantly renewed through new conquests. If she feels it's enough of a problem, she would probably be helped by some form of psychotherapy, rather than sex therapy, because it appears to me that her sexual behavior has to do with her personality in general.

SEX THERAPY

How do I know whether I should go to a regular psychotherapist or to a sex therapist for my sexual problem?

It depends upon how direct and concrete you want to be in approaching the problem. A sex therapist will usually deal with it as primarily a sexual problem. A "regular therapist," or generalist, may not. He or she may, in the course of discussing your sexual problem, uncover many other problems, such as unassertiveness or depression, and feel it best to work on your sexual problem by dealing with those. The generalist will usually attempt a broader change in your personality rather than a direct change only in your sexuality. However, sometimes there is a cross-referral during the course of the therapy. Sex therapists and generalists both refer patients to each other whenever that seems appropriate, either as an alternative or an adjunct.

What really happens during sex therapy?

The techniques and approaches used depend upon the specific problem being treated. For example:

• *Information about Sexuality* Occasionally the source of a person's sexual difficulties is simply a lack of proper information. In these few cases, the therapeutic task is fairly easy, in that your therapist corrects any misconceptions and provides you with information and encouragement.

• *Sexual History and Analysis* of your sexual dysfunction help both the therapist and you to understand the underlying psychological difficulty that is causing your sexual problem. For example, your family may have been strongly antisexual. This has caused you as an adult to feel that sex is shameful and dirty, which makes you feel inhibited. Or you may have been trained by society—your church, school, friends, TV and movies—to inhibit your sexuality.

• *Challenging Your Antisexual Attitudes and Your Fear of Loss of Control* By making you aware that this is what is going on in your head around the issues of sexuality, you can be helped to consciously refute some of these thoughts. In addition, most often sexual problems are aggravated by the pressure that people place on themselves in regard to sexual performance. The therapist will also help you to understand and challenge your perfectionism in regard to sexuality, and to create situations in which there is the least amount of pressure.

• *A Wide Range of Behavioral Techniques* The sex therapist may focus on homework—exercises you do outside the session, frequently with your sexual partner, in order to reorient you toward sexuality. The therapist might begin therapy with homework that involves you and your partner using foreplay more creatively to enhance the level of arousal. "Sensate focus," developed by Masters and Johnson, is a series of graduated steps of sexual contact between sexual partners within which the individual learns to tune in to sexual excitement as opposed to sexual anxieties and inhibitions. If the issue is the loss of control in the presence of another person, the therapist might begin with homework that involves your gradually exposing more of your emotions to others.

What about having sexual surrogates? Isn't that like going to a prostitute?

No, it's not. Some therapists feel that sexual surrogates may sometimes be a necessary part of the therapy if the person in therapy has no partner to work with. A surrogate is a person who has been specially trained, and who proceeds in a step-by-step manner that the sexual therapist prescribes. You feel relaxed with the surrogate and gradually improve in sexual confidence and performance.

Although there has been a lot of controversy over the morality of using sexual surrogates, there is another problem with this approach. Some point out that it is too artificial a situation and is not adequate preparation for making the jump to a nonpaid partner. My own opinion is somewhat negative toward surrogates. I don't think that they should *never* be used, but that they are a last resort if a suitable partner can't be found. If the person truly has no social contacts, the therapy should probably start with working on *that* problem.

Why do people have so many sexual problems? Is there any general advice you can give to people who want to try to solve their sexual problems on their own?

Sexual problems are usually caused by feelings of inhibition and pressure. We're all born with sexuality, but we've been raised to be inhibited about it. The greatest problem in sexuality is that it's not talked about, and the best self-help advice I can give you is to create a relationship in which you and your partner can be very open and honest about your sexuality. Whatever the specific complaint, talking about it in a relaxed, safe environment tends to decrease pressure and inhibition. Communication is one very important key.

In my experience, people feel a great deal of conflict about sexuality because of the sometimes conflicting messages they receive. On the one hand, we are taught much shame and guilt about our own sexuality, an ongoing experience known as antisexuality. On the other hand, the media stress our sexuality. I think that the focus on sex as the key point in romantic love is overstressed and overdone. People are led to believe that if a sexual experience is not as steamy, passionate, or frequent as portrayed in the movies and in advertising that there is something wrong with the relationship. In addition, people have learned to equate a certain standard of physical attractiveness with good sex. This is an enormous mistake, because it unfairly rules out most people who do not fit this stereotype as "not sexy," which is not true.

CHAPTER FOURTEEN

Uncontrolled Thoughts and Actions

COMPULSIONS

I can't leave the house until everything is perfectly clean and in order. My fussing keeps everybody waiting and makes them angry. Isn't it good to be neat and clean?

Most people feel some need to be neat, some people more than others. But in your case it sounds like too much of a good thing. Your need to be neat has become compulsive because you say you "can't" leave the house. Neatness has gotten in the way of your relationships with other people and your other activities.

I don't remember being overly neat and clean, although my mother was always after me to clean my room. So why is it that I have become compulsively neat?

There are at least three possible mechanisms at work in your case.

• People often become compulsively neat because they have been directly trained in an extreme way that they must do things just right or to be neat, above all. Perhaps your mother's nagging affected you more than you realize.

• You may be acting in a passive-aggressive manner— asserting control over other people by refusing to give in to their time requirements, rather than telling them directly when you would like to leave or what you would like to do.

• In addition, you may be using your compulsion to preoccupy yourself in order to avoid thinking of other things or to avoid other emotional experiences. When you're thinking of dust all the time, you're less likely to feel and to have painful thoughts enter your mind. A woman patient of mine was constantly arranging and rearranging the glasses in her kitchen closets during the time she was going through a difficult divorce. Some people work hard at keeping their desks and files scrupulously clean and in order; this, of course, leaves less time for them to worry about the quality of their work.

My compulsiveness is driving me crazy. Everything takes so long and I get so aggravated with myself. What can I do on my own to stop this compulsive behavior?

The simplest self-treatment is to limit the time you devote to your compulsive activity. Tell yourself, "I'm only going to clean and straighten today for three hours." Then gradually reduce this time until it is down to some level at which it allows you much more freedom. If this approach doesn't work for you, therapy will help you uncover the causes of your behavior.

OBSESSIONS

Lately I've been thinking about a high school boyfriend, and I can't get him out of my mind. I'm worried that this will affect my marriage.

Any thought that you have over and over again and that won't go away—even though you want it to—is an obsession. I believe that with an obsession, your mind is playing a trick on you. In your case, your mind is telling you that this former boyfriend is the ultimate in desirability. However, this is probably not the case—rather, there is something in your present life that is bringing this memory on.

But why should I suddenly become obsessed by these thoughts? How can I stop them?

Your obsession may arise out of any number of unconscious motives. For example, you may feel anger toward your husband, but you are not letting yourself experience or express this directly. Thinking about your former boyfriend may offer something that your husband does not—such as a need for tenderness which you may not be aware of.

Here are three techniques you might want to try to help you stop these thoughts:

1. You can begin by picking apart in your mind why this fellow is coming to mind. I call this going underneath the obsession, and it is frequently hard to accomplish. If you are able to come up with a satisfying answer, see what you can change in your life to make it more agreeable.

2. You can also try a behavioral technique called "thought stopping." When your former boyfriend does come into your mind, distract yourself and don't allow yourself to dwell and fantasize. You may mentally tell yourself to "stop," or even say it out loud if circumstances permit. This may help somewhat, although this technique sometimes backfires—when you try too hard to push a thought out of your mind, it can come roaring back in.

3. Another approach is to allow thoughts of him to drift into your mind, but to not take them seriously. You may find that by not fighting them or worrying about them, they will go away of their own accord.

If you go to a therapist, he or she will try to help you puzzle out why these obsessive thoughts are coming to you right now. An obsession usually has some significance that is much more meaningful than it appears on the surface, and a therapist can help you understand this.

I am always worried that someday I'm going to die, especially since I know it's true. It's hard for me to understand how other people can take it so calmly. Why am I like this?

The interesting point in this question is that death is not a fantasized fear: No one lives forever, and we all will die sometime. The fear of death is almost universal—when death approaches, almost no one wants to die—but the difference here is that not everyone is obsessive about it.

There must be some special reason why death is staying on your mind. Such obsessions have many causes. I have treated a number of people with this same obsession. Two underlying ideas seem to stand out in these cases:

• The first is the feeling of being cheated out of life—in other words, never having fully *lived*. People who feel this way are perpetually putting off pleasures or feeling downtrodden and are envious of others who seem to be enjoying their lives. The thought of death is totally unacceptable to these people because it would mean accepting having had a life without real enjoyment. It is my belief that when you can't accept something, it stays on your mind.

• The second involves people who are always dreading that they are going to die by means of some horrible disease or accident. It is my belief that these people unconsciously believe they deserve such a fate. This type of death is unacceptable to them not only because it cheats them of life, but because the possibility of it reaffirms their belief that they are bad. This lack of acceptance again accounts for their obsessive thinking about death.

Sometimes this type of obsession occurs only occasionally, and is not really too worrisome. Perhaps your obsession with death will respond to reassurance from others or to self-reassurance. If not, I recommend psychotherapy to work through the underlying problem that keeps your obsessive thoughts going.

I'm very worried about the threat of nuclear war. I see this in my children too, and we talk about it a lot. How can we learn to live with this horrible possibility?

If the threat of nuclear annihilation preoccupies you and prevents you from enjoying life, you should be concerned. There may be a psychological issue surrounding your obsession which may respond to therapy.

On the other hand, if you are simply aware that there is a nuclear threat, rest assured it really *ought* to be on your mind to a certain extent. The best way to handle this natural concern is to turn it into action. Don't be passive—worry is passive! Action reduces worry. So get out there and become involved in whatever particular form of action suits you.

HYPOCHONDRIA

I'm always thinking that I've got cancer. My doctor reassures me that I'm okay, but a few weeks later I'm sure that I'm sick again. Even if I'm healthy now, I can't stop thinking that I'm going to get cancer.

Yes, you're right in that no one can assure you 100 percent that you don't have cancer now, or won't get it sometime in the future. Yet why does it prey on your mind and not on the minds of most other people? There may be a wide range of reasons:

• Your parents might have trained you to be afraid of disease, and you may have latched onto cancer in particular because it's being widely discussed in the media.

• You may in some way be punishing yourself because you believe you deserve to be sick.

• You may be using the preoccupation as a means to get attention from doctors because you're not getting the attention you need at home.

• You may be using this means to distract yourself from other unpleasant thoughts, such as problems with your spouse, or to control other people in your environment.

In general, people who are hypochondriacs should go into therapy because they truly are suffering and no amount of

155

reassurances from a medical doctor seems to solve the problem.

Whenever I get nervous, my skin acts up. My doctor says that it's psychosomatic, but my friends call me a hypochondriac. What is the difference between hypochondria and psychosomatic disorders?

Hypochondriacs may have some minor physical sensations, but what they really focus on is the worry that they are ill. They imagine that they are ill, or that they are going to get ill. In psychosomatic disease, there is a measurable physical disturbance. The mental state is at least partly responsible for the headache, ulcer, or in your case the skin rash. A person who is psychosomatic may not be dwelling on the psychological or physical problem per se and often ignores or denies that there is any psychological connection at all. (See Chapter 15 for information about psychosomatic disorders.)

PROCRASTINATION AND INDECISION

I tend to put off making decisions until the last minute, and when I have to make them, I agonize until I actually choose something. Is this a problem I need help with?

As you may know, you have plenty of company in your problem. It's natural for many people to put off things that will be difficult or unpleasant. Making major decisions requires time and careful consideration, and we frequently have at least some trouble with them. In fact, you may wrongly admire people who are able to make snap decisions. These people may be afraid of examining things, of being in a state of indecisiveness and conflict, and therefore act rashly.

To determine whether indecisiveness is a problem in your life, ask yourself these three questions:

1. Do I spend a great deal of time and energy being indecisive over small, inconsequential things?
2. Do I put off making major decisions indefinitely?
3. Do I refuse to make decisions and let time—or other people—make the decisions for me?

If you can answer "yes" to one or more of these questions, then this pattern of behavior is a problem that could be worked on.

I can't decide whether I should change jobs. I've been agonizing over it for years, and my friends criticize me for procrastinating. Is procrastination the same as indecisiveness?

Although they have elements in common, they feel somewhat different to the person experiencing them. When you're procrastinating, you clearly know and believe that you should follow a particular direction. However, somehow you don't follow that direction. Procrastination is an experience of postponement and delay, of inertia and inactivity. If you are procrastinating, you are probably very confused and might say, "I know what to do—I don't understand why I don't just do it." If you are being indecisive, on the other hand, you feel, "I don't know what to do—I just can't make up my mind."

Sometimes what looks like indecisiveness or procrastination really isn't—if, for instance, you wish you had a car but you delay buying one because you have to spend the money on your rent. In this case, *you* are not actually preventing yourself from buying a car—real-life conditions and/or necessary expenses are making it impossible.

I feel stuck in many places in my life. Sometimes I put off doing the smallest thing and can never decide what is right for me. I'm so jealous of people who are not like this. Why do I have this problem with indecision and procrastination?

Like most procrastinators and indecisive people, you probably feel some underlying dread of doing it wrong. It's always possible to make a mistake, but you tend to be in perpetual doubt about yourself. Consequently, you no sooner start going in one direction than you turn around and pull in another, worrying that you have made the wrong choice. You probably also exaggerate the consequences of making a wrong decision. Procrastination allows you to say "no" to somebody without directly confronting them, and to avoid taking responsibility for your own actions.

Although procrastination is itself unpleasant, it is a frequent form of escape from something you find even more unpleasant. Procrastinators are often perfectionists—very demanding of themselves. You tend to put yourself under the stress of having to do an impossibly perfect job, work hard to not make any mistakes, and chastise yourself when you do a less-than-perfect job. Under such mental self-torture it seems better to you to not attempt things at all, or to put off doing them until the last possible moment, and so have an excuse for falling short of perfection.

Oddly enough, procrastinators can also put off doing some absolutely pleasant things for themselves. In this case, the psychological situation is quite different. These people believe that they don't deserve the pleasantness, or they fear that somehow they will be punished for treating themselves too well. I have several patients with successful careers who procrastinate endlessly whenever it's time to enjoy the fruits of their labors.

What can I do on my own to stop procrastinating or being indecisive?

When severe, these problems are frequently really part of a complex thought pattern that is believed to have very deep roots in a person's past. What usually doesn't work is subjecting yourself to even more self-pressure to act, or making endless plus-and-minus lists to reach a decision. Rather, try following these approaches:

1. The first thing you can do is to try to recognize the

underlying causes. For example, see if the real reason you put off painting your apartment is because of your perfectionism. If so, you may be able to realize that it doesn't *have* to be perfect—that having it done reasonably well is better than not having it done at all. Try not to confuse doing the best that *you* can with doing the best that *anybody* can.

2. Try cutting a large task down into smaller tasks that can be done one at a time. That way, you aren't overwhelmed by facing the entire task at once. If the task is truly unpleasant, you can focus on the more pleasant feeling of accomplishment that follows.

3. Another approach that works well, particularly for tasks that require mental concentration such as studying, is to train yourself to focus on task-relevant thoughts. Don't allow any daydreaming, or outside thoughts, to intrude. You do this by setting a kitchen timer for short periods of time—two to five minutes—then starting to work. When the bell goes off, notice what you're thinking. If it's task-relevant, give yourself a check mark; if it's extraneous, give yourself an X. At the end of your work period, total them up. If you have too many X's, try again, but cut the periods shorter. Then gradually lengthen the periods of time until you no longer need the timer.

4. Try this "first-thought" exercise: As soon as you think of doing something, do it *immediately*—not in a minute, not in an hour, and not tomorrow. By training yourself to act impulsively, you short-circuit that feeling of dread and the procrastination it brings.

5. If you are having trouble making a decision, try to recognize your dread of making a mistake. Recognize that even the wrong decision won't be as bad as you imagine it will be. It might also help to look for more information on the issue, or to try to discover additional options that may be more acceptable than the ones you are currently considering.

How do I know when I should have therapy for procrastination and indecision?

SHOULD YOU HAVE PSYCHOTHERAPY?

I recommend psychotherapy if your indecision and procrastination involve many situations; or if your trouble with a
specific issue drags on for a long time; or if you find it causes
you a lot of discomfort, even if you're functioning well in
other areas of your life. If self-help has been only minimally
effective, or if you find yourself procrastinating in regard to
even the self-help suggestions, I think it would be worthwhile
for you to explore psychotherapy. Finally, if you are chronically indecisive about entering therapy, then I would say you
probably should go.

CHAPTER FIFTEEN

Psychosomatic Disorders

I've never understood what "psychosomatic" means. Is it the same as when people imagine that they are sick?

No. When people continually *imagine* that they are sick, we use the term "hypochondriac." When you have a psychosomatic disorder, your psychological state interacts with an already existing biological tendency, probably inherited, to give your body a particular disorder. Some common examples of this include ulcers and functional colitis. If your body is prone to a particular disorder or illness, your psychological state can make it worse.

I've suffered from ulcers for five years now. I've changed my diet, and my doctor has treated me with all kinds of drugs for my stomach. But nothing seems to help very much. Now he tells me that a lot of my problem is in my head. But the pain is real, isn't it?

Yes, the pain and the ulcer are real. What your doctor is telling you is that certain psychological factors are at work to keep your stomach in turmoil, which sabotages his attempts to treat you medically. Many physical sensations—and even observable physical changes such as ulcers—can have both physical and psychological causes. In no way does this make the ulcer any less real than it would be if it were caused by nonpsychological means. Of course, it is necessary for your doctor to continue to treat you for the physical disorder that is present in your stomach. However, it would appear that you would also benefit from psychotherapy to help work out the psychological problems that may be contributing to or aggravating your physical problem.

I don't understand. How does my thinking or feeling a certain way about something cause these physical changes?

Many mental states produce emotions that cause physiological changes. For example, in the case of ulcers, the mental state of anxiety is accompanied by proliferating stomach acid, which in turn produces a hole in the stomach. Experts in this area believe that in disorders of this kind there is a biological tendency toward a particular disorder and the psychological state can determine whether the symptoms will appear.

I frequently get headaches, especially after a really tense day at work. My doctor says there's nothing wrong with me physically. Could my problem be psychological?

Yes, in a way. In fact the most common type of headache is called a "tension headache." To begin with, you probably come from a family in which people are predisposed to have tension "go to" the head muscles. When you get tense, given this predisposition, you then get a "tension headache." The problem lies in your chronically getting tense when demands that you doubt you can meet are made upon you at work. This tension then produces the headache.

You can try to alleviate your problem on your own by using relaxation tapes and books, by learning to meditate, or by engaging in regular exercise. If these self-help approaches don't do the trick, it is probably best if you explore the source of your tension with a psychotherapist. Biofeedback, a technique often used by psychotherapists to treat psychosomatic disorders by teaching patients how to relax muscles, has been found to be a very effective means of direct treatment of headaches, and that may be all that's needed. If not, broader-based, long-term therapy may be needed to gain a greater understanding of what the tension is all about. Sometimes these two approaches are used simultaneously with good results.

I'm so nervous that my bad back is beginning to act up. My doctor gave me a prescription for something to calm me down. But I don't want to take tranquilizers—can psychotherapy help?

Yes, it's certainly worth a try. Although it sounds as though your doctor is acknowledging the psychological aspects of your physical problem, it also sounds as though he may believe more strongly in the continued use of tranquilizers than in psychotherapy as a solution. You certainly should discuss your reservations about tranquilizers with him and express your interest in psychotherapy as an alternative solution. If you do enter therapy, it will be important to have your therapist and physician in contact with each other, particularly if you are on medication, since the dosage may need to be adjusted.

CHAPTER SIXTEEN

Crises

DEATH

I was married for twenty-seven years and my husband died four months ago. I still feel so lost without him. Is this normal?

Yes, it certainly is. The best way to deal with your grief is to let yourself fully experience the loss and the loneliness that the death of someone so close to you brings. If you let your mourning be short-circuited by well-meaning friends and relatives who are trying to cheer you up, it tends to linger on, sometimes in disguised forms. So it's best to let this experience have its full vent.

What if my sense of grief never goes away, years after the death of someone close?

If your grief never seems to decrease, but lingers and becomes very obsessive, look for a reason. You may be obsessive about the past out of a fear of starting to deal with the present and the future. This holding onto a past event protects you from having to confront life and start up again. It is also possible that you have always been frightened of being on your own—and that this issue was solved by your marrying your husband. Now that he's gone, there's no one for you to depend on.

Or it may be that a sense of guilt is bothering you. You may feel guilty that you lived and that your husband died, or that you weren't as nice to him as you might have been while he was alive. I had a patient, a teen-age girl, who had a fight with her grandmother during which she yelled at her, "Why don't you drop dead!" A day or two later, the grandmother died. The girl had had a very close relationship with her grandmother, and she felt very guilty.

If grief lingers so long that it prevents you from having a satisfying life, you're probably hiding behind it or stuck with it for some underlying reason. You may want to explore with a therapist what your fears are all about.

DIVORCE

My wife and I are getting a divorce and I feel very angry with her. How can I keep from feeling this way? I don't want to ruin my relationship with my children.

It's expected that anger will be generated in a divorce. After all, one or both partners have been hurt and disappointed. You may feel that you shouldn't allow yourself to feel angry at all because this emotion has always been difficult for you to admit or express, or you may feel guilty about getting the divorce in the first place.

It is hard to imagine a divorce without any anger, so it is certainly all right to feel it and express it in a physically harmless and legal way which doesn't involve the children. You can express it directly to your wife; if this is impractical, you can write a letter; if that is also impractical, tell it to a friend. You don't have to suppress anger. When emotions are suppressed, they tend to linger for a long time.

I've developed a bad habit since my divorce. After my kids visit their father, I can't stop myself from putting him down to them. How can I stop myself from doing this?

You can begin by realizing you are putting the kids in the middle of a terrible conflict. Do you *really* want them to hate their father? You may feel the need to do this for several possible reasons:

• You are not expressing your anger to the most appropriate person (your former husband). Instead, you put on a false facade and express your anger indirectly by putting him down to your children.

• You feel doubtful and insecure about your position and so need to muster allies (your children). Perhaps you can become more aware that your own thoughts and feelings about the marriage are worth expressing—you don't really need the alliance of your children to lodge a complaint against your husband.

• You are feeling guilty that you caused the children pain, and so to justify the divorce you are trying to get them to align themselves with you. Although of course they did feel pain at the breakup of the family, remember that, in most cases, children suffer more from a rotten marriage than from a good divorce.

I compare everyone I go out with to my former wife and end up thinking they're not as great as she was. My friends tell me this is very destructive. Will I ever get over my wife?

Depending upon how long it's been since the breakup, it's natural to do some comparing. On the other hand, too much comparing can be seen as a protective device. You may be trying to avoid being open to establishing a new relationship and the vulnerability that goes along with it. You may still be hooked on your former wife, idolizing her and the marriage in an unrealistic way. You must learn to face the fact that none of these people will ever be your former wife, and that by idolizing a situation from the past which no longer really exists for you, you are being unfair to others and to yourself. People should not be judged by holding them up to comparison with other people, but according to what your experience is with them as individuals in their own right.

ILLNESS

I've been taking care of my ailing mother for years. Now I find I'm becoming bitter toward my brothers and sisters who live out of town. What should I do?

It sounds as though you're feeling overly burdened with responsibilities, and that somehow, either because of your own personality traits or circumstances beyond your control, you've been forced into shouldering this obligation. You should begin to reduce your responsibility either by attempting to get your brothers and sisters to visit at times, or by having them contribute financially to the hiring of someone who can take over for you at times. If this is not possible, at least let your brothers and sisters know about your resentment.

I just found out I have cancer. I feel so shocked and helpless. I've never been sick a day in my life, and now I have to face the fact that I may soon die. Will therapy help me cope better?

Yes, if you go to the right therapist—someone who has expertise in helping people who are facing this kind of crisis. Therapy in this instance is usually short-term. People generally may not require extensive treatment in order to get back on their feet emotionally, although they may find that they require follow-up visits during the course of their illness and perhaps even after recovery.

In addition, or alternatively, you might find it very helpful to join a support group where other people with cancer can share with you their feelings and experiences, and help give you the sense that you are not alone. The National Cancer Institute's Cancer Information Service and the American Cancer Society will help you locate support groups; in addition, several cities have established special "hot lines" which allow you to talk one-on-one with another cancer patient or an experienced mental health worker. These alternatives may work in conjunction with therapy or in place of it.

Cancer patients must struggle with issues that can seem overwhelming. At times you may feel alienated, afraid of being abandoned, unaccepted, and isolated. You may feel mutilated from the medical treatment. You must come face to face with your own mortality. At various times you may have feelings of vulnerability, helplessness, and loss of control over your body and your life. In general, people who have cancer or any other serious illness tend to be too stoic and brave. But you shouldn't hesitate to ask for help to get you through this difficult, highly stressful period.

LOSS OF JOB

I just lost my job and I feel absolutely devastated—so lost and insecure. I wonder if I can get any help, or is this just the way things have to be?

Most people feel lost and insecure when they lose their jobs. Our job is usually one of the mainstays of our lives and when that changes—and it can change very suddenly—most of us feel a great loss in terms of status, income, and what to do with our time. So your type of reaction is not unusual. If, however, your reaction is so severe that it prevents you from functioning—if, for instance, you can't even look for another job—or if the period of unemployment is very long, it might be helpful to involve yourself in some kind of therapy. In this case, a group therapy model might be more appropriate than individual therapy, although both should be considered.

I know it wasn't my fault that I lost my job, and I know I'll get another job eventually, so why am I ashamed to tell my family about it?

What you're really saying here is that the shame is causing you pain, and what should you do about the shame? My guess is that there's a great deal of self-blame going on here.

You are saying, "I deserved to lose my job." Take a few minutes to examine this thought—did you *really* deserve to lose your job? Or was it actually a combination of factors, some of which were at least partially out of your control?

If the worst possibility is true—that you did deserve to lose your job, ask yourself: Don't I have the right to be wrong? Because you did badly at this job doesn't mean you'll always do badly or that you're a worthless person. And even though you are jobless, your family will most likely still love you and accept you. But more important, you can surely still love yourself.

CRIME VICTIM

A while ago, my house was broken into and everything was stolen. Now, every time I get near my home, I feel afraid that it's been broken into again. How long will this feeling go on?

Your feelings are certainly understandable, as anyone whose home has been broken into knows. It's a very frightening experience to have gone through, and your type of response can be expected to last for some period of time. If it persists, or if it really upsets you, this may be caused by an underlying fear in general of being hurt, an underlying sense of deserving to have bad things happen to you. I predict a fairly rapid decrease in your feelings of fear as you see that your house is not broken into again.

I was raped by someone I knew slightly. I never told anyone. I'm so ashamed and confused. He said I asked for it. Can psychotherapy help me?

Yes, especially if you are able to find a therapist who has had special training in treating rape victims. Rape is a traumatic experience; it is normal for you to have feelings of powerlessness and of having been physically invaded. Many women have nightmares or insomnia after having been raped.

Some feel guilty that they may have somehow caused it, or that they didn't do enough to prevent it. Rape victims sometimes feel anger and distrust toward all men, and they may have sexual problems afterward.

As is the case with all crimes of violence, some victims recover quickly, but others may take a very long time to put the experience behind them. Even so, there are resources to which you can turn which will help you learn to cope. Rape crisis hot lines will put you in touch with trained counselors who will offer you the support you need at this time. Many hospitals have special rape victim treatment programs that combine physical and psychological treatment. Alternatively, you may be able to turn to your private physician for support. If you are having trouble coping, and especially if that difficulty persists, locate the nearest antirape advocacy group or women's center in your area and ask for a referral to a therapist who specializes in rape cases.

CHAPTER SEVENTEEN

Psychoses

My friend's mother, whom we've always considered eccentric, started acting stranger and stranger. She was finally convinced that she should go to a therapist, and two weeks later she was in a hospital. Why are some conditions treated in a hospital rather than in a psychotherapist's office?

Hospitalization is usually seen as a last resort and is considered only when outpatient therapy is not adequate to protect the person or society, or cannot achieve the desired goals of the therapy. Psychotic patients may need to be treated in an institutional setting because they require a great deal of supervision and care. In addition, they sometimes need to be stabilized on very strong drugs; that requires a staff to observe the patient, administer the drugs, and protect the patient from himself or herself, or to protect others from the patient.

What is a psychosis? How do you know when a person is psychotic?

People with psychoses have lost contact with reality, or at least with some segment of it. This loss is evidenced by the presence of bizarre behavior and the inability to function in important areas in the person's life. It is a very serious form of mental illness.

In some psychotic patients we see a wide range of inappropriate emotions from rage to despair. Many, however, seem emotionally flat, apparently unaffected by the world around them. Their symptoms include delusions, hallucinations, incoherent speech, frozen body posture, hyperactivity, psychotic (very severe) depression, bizarre dress, a disruption of personal hygiene, and a wide range of other symptoms which, to the untrained observer, always seem strange and inexplicable.

Most psychotics are unaware of their condition, and must be persuaded or forced to seek help. Some psychotic conditions seem chronic, and once a person has the first psychotic episode, he or she never regains full functioning. Others, however, particularly since the development of antipsychotic medication, have relatively short psychotic episodes and hospitalization, after which they return to full lives.

On TV the other night, I saw a movie about a woman who they said was schizophrenic. Is schizophrenia the same as being psychotic?

Psychosis is an umbrella category which includes several types of disorders. Schizophrenia is the most common of these, and many consider it to have the poorest prognosis.

Sometimes I act so differently when I'm around different people that I think I have a split personality. Am I schizophrenic?

It is a misconception that schizophrenics have split personalities. The term originally was used to refer to the "splitting off" of thoughts from one another. A schizophrenic's thoughts neither flow smoothly nor follow one another logically, and that is why their conversations can at times seem incoherent to us. Therefore, even though you say you change dramatically, I don't think this indicates that you are a schizophrenic.

Schizophrenia is a complex disorder that usually affects all aspects of a person's personality. Symptoms usually begin during the early twenties to early thirties; occasionally, some cases develop in childhood or later in life. Prior to the actual onset of the psychotic symptoms, these individuals are frequently somewhat eccentric and somewhat antisocial. However, the onset sometimes strikes suddenly in a person who up to then seemed normal and healthy. Within the category of schizophrenia, there are many subcategories. For example, a person may be a paranoid schizophrenic who has delusions that other people are dangerous enemies. Catatonic schizophrenics withdraw from their surroundings so completely that they become mute or stare motionlessly into space for hours.

We are still not sure of the causes of schizophrenia; some believe that it results from emotional and/or psychological causes; others think that biochemistry and an inherited predisposition are involved. Most thinking now revolves around the probability that it comes from a combination of genetic and environmental factors which interact with each other.

I worry about my moods—sometimes I'm very up, but at other times I feel very down. Is this manic depression?

It may be, but many people experience mild mood swings without being manic-depressive. A less common form of psychotic disorder with a better prognosis than schizophrenia, manic-depressive psychosis is, in many cases, completely controlled by medication. In this disorder, people may experience *severe* moods. Most commonly, the mood is one of depression. Some individuals, however, suffer periods of mania, marked by unrealistic expansiveness and amazing energy. Occasionally, individuals swing between these two moods.

My sister has just tried to commit suicide and is threatening to try it again. How do I know whether her threats are serious?

Her threats *are* serious in that almost all suicide threats should be taken seriously, if not literally. What I mean by this is that the person who says she is going to kill herself may not intend to do it this week, or this month, but it is on her mind for some reason and some time from now it may actually happen.

Many people let other people know that they are having these thoughts as a means of calling for help. Bearing this in mind, I'm surprised that your sister has not entered therapy already. She should certainly be urged to see a professional. Once your sister is in therapy, you can certainly be helpful in supplying the encouragement and support that your sister needs to confront her problems. Do not give your sister or yourself the impression that you are going to take responsibility for her care. Be sure to communicate to her that, as much as you love her, you are not trained to be her therapist.

Sometimes I think about committing suicide. Does this mean I'm a psychotic?

Not necessarily. Thoughts of suicide may be a sign of depression and/or an indirect way of expressing hostility. Some psychotics may end up killing themselves—they may jump off a bridge because they believe that they can fly, or that the devil makes them do it. This is not the same as the depressed person who wants to end it all because life doesn't seem worth living or in order to show close friends and family how mistreated the person feels.

A friend of mine needs mental care. If she is sent to an institution, how will she be treated?

At one time, people were kept in mental institutions for very long periods of time. Today, the accent is on discharging patients as soon as possible—with short-term crisis-type treatment and stabilizing medication—so it's not likely that your relative will be kept for an inordinate amount of time.

In addition, in the past, institutions were very demeaning to patients; they were not seen as people who had rights. But the new state and federal guidelines are making it much more common for these institutions to attempt to normalize people's lives while they are in the hospital, providing them with at least the rudiments of what are considered to be the rights and privileges of adults.

This information should allay your fears to some degree, but I advise you to still keep a watchful eye out to ensure that these rights are being respected by the institution and that your friend is getting the best possible therapy. If not, there are many channels through which you can make your objections known.

My brother has had some mental problems in the past and is about to be released from a mental hospital. How do I know he won't be dangerous?

The vast majority of people who have been hospitalized are not dangerous. Most patients in mental hospitals are there because they are not able to function in the world; they just can't take care of themselves. While this inability may have caused him and others some discomfort, it is not necessarily dangerous. The best way for you to allay your fears is to consult with the discharging physician to find out what problems your brother may face in adjusting to living outside. This is usually best done before he is released.

What can I do to help my brother after he is discharged from the hospital?

This depends greatly on the kind of difficulties he has. Usually people who have been released from psychiatric hospitals are stabilized on medication, and it's probably important for you to support his taking his medication regularly as prescribed. Most people respond positively to a supportive, sometimes moderately structured, environment. If you can help provide some regular social interaction and other pleasurable activities as well as some kind of productive work (if appropriate), it would be a big help. In other words, your brother needs to live a life as close as possible to normal, but with a bit more structure and encouragement, and possibly a bit more tolerance toward eccentricity.

Should I talk about his problems and hospitalization?

SHOULD YOU HAVE PSYCHOTHERAPY?

This is a difficult question to answer because it depends upon so many different factors. Your brother may be the type of person who is so obsessive that talking about it may drive him back into the obsessive aspect of his illness. On the other hand, it may be that your talking about it will show him that you recognize that there is nothing shameful in what he has gone through. You can let him know that you realize that people can suffer from mental disorders and come out of it, that it's okay and why not talk about it?